Beyond the Horizon
Frontiers for Mission

Edited by
Charles R. Henery

**The Jackson Kemper Conference
Nashotah House
1985**

JACKSON KEMPER

And this is what is meant by a MISSIONARY BISHOP—a Bishop sent forth by the Church, not sought for of the Church—going before to organize the Church, not waiting till the Church has partially been organized—a leader, not a follower, in the march of the Redeemer's conquering and triumphant Gospel—sent by the Church, even as the Church is sent by Christ.

> — *Sermon Preached at the Consecration of Jackson Kemper by the Rt. Rev. George W. Doane, Bishop of New Jersey, September 25, 1835.*

Preface

In 1835 the Episcopal Church in the United States charted a new and bold missionary course. That year, in General Convention, the Church formally constituted itself a missionary community, naming all the baptized within its household as members of the Domestic and Foreign Missionary Society and charging them with responsibility to carry forward the work of missions in the world. The measure was adopted out of an urgent sense of need for corporate and united action in missionary expansion at home and abroad. The new policy recognized that mission is not the special interest of a group within the Church, but the concern of the whole Church. Thus it aimed to recover the primitive understanding of the Church as an apostolic company, a fellowship of men and women who have been called and commissioned in baptism to a ministry of witness and service to Christ.

The pathfinder for this new missionary venture of the Episcopal Church on the American frontier was Jackson Kemper. Born near Poughkeepsie in 1789, a graduate of Columbia College and a disciple of the dynamic Bishop John Henry Hobart of New York, under whom he studied theology, Kemper was one of the early figures in the Church who saw clearly the missionary challenge presented in the young growing Republic.

From the day of his ordination to the diaconate, in 1811, Kemper vigorously pushed the cause of western missions. Serving as assistant minister to Bishop William White in the United Parish of Philadelphia, he led in the formation of a diocesan missionary society in Pennsylvania and accepted assignment as its first missionary, making several trips over the years to the infant communities beyond the Alleghenies. In the General Convention of 1820 he was prominent among those who successfully promoted the establishment of a national missionary society, acting as a director of the new voluntary organization and consigning a great portion of his time and energies to enlisting support for its work. Later in 1834, three years after becoming rector of St. Paul's Church, Norwalk, Connecticut, he traveled on behalf of the national society to investigate the Indian mission at Green Bay, then in Michigan territory.

Jackson Kemper was a born missionary. And the Church realized this when it called him to become the first missionary bishop in America. Consecrated on September 25, 1835, he was given initial oversight of Indiana and Missouri, but his jurisdiction soon grew to include the territories of Wisconsin, Iowa, Minnesota, Kansas and Nebraska. It was a vast missionary field, yet Bishop Kemper proved himself more than equal to the charge. For twenty-four years he tirelessly ranged the land, preaching, baptizing, confirming, and planting missions. When at length in 1859 he resigned his missionary office to devote his remaining years as diocesan bishop of Wisconsin, Kemper had laid the deep and permanent foundation of his prayers for the Church in the West. Where once there had been no organized diocese, at his death there were seven hardy and growing dioceses in the nation's heartland, each with its own bishop, and he the father of them all.

Jackson Kemper died on May 24, 1870, at his home in Delafield, Wisconsin. He was buried in the nearby cemetery of Nashotah House, the missionary seminary whose foundation he inspired. To the last he remained the faithful apostle, never faltering in his devotion or straying from the path of duty. No man had done more to advance the Church's mission in this land and to foster the understanding of the episcopate as a missionary office. As Bishop Thomas Vail of Kansas said at Kemper's funeral: "His life furnishes a most important link, not only in the history of our American Church but in the history of the Church Catholic of this age, as it develops its grand missionary work for the benefit of the world."

To commemorate the 150th anniversary of the consecration of Jackson Kemper as the Episcopal Church's first missionary bishop, Nashotah House held a national conference September 26-28, 1985, on the theme "A Missionary Church." Over 170 persons, representing some 44 dioceses and including 18 bishops, gathered with members of the Nashotah community for this three-day conference to hear a number of distinguished Church leaders and scholars reassess the missionary vocation of the Episcopal Church. This book comprises the addresses and sermons delivered at the conference. They will be found, it is believed, to offer not only a valuable perspective on the past missionary work of the Episcopal Church in America, but to point as well to the missionary challenges before the Church at present and in the future.

Today, as in 1835, the Episcopal Church is called to reaffirm its missionary character and to recognize the critical mission frontiers in society. There is still the need in our Christian household for us, as former Presiding Bishop John Maury Allin told the conference, "to refocus, clarify and enlarge our missionary perspective." But what this requires, Bishop Allin reminds us, is that we look beyond the limited horizon of our own personal, parochial or diocesan interests and acknowledge the duty that is ours. It is hoped that this book will contribute to that larger, fuller vision of mission, and together we might look *beyond the horizon* and set forth anew on our unfinished course of witnessing to the Good News of God in Christ.

As chairman of the Kemper anniversary conference, I would like to thank the trustees, the dean and faculty, and all the members of the Nashotah House community, as well as the many friends whose names appear in this book, for their support and sponsorship of the conference. My special thanks go to Peter L. Ingeman, Walter L. Prehn III, Timothy L. Anderson, John L. Hartnett, J. Connor Haynes, Robert B. Slocum, LeGrand A. Van Keuren Jr. and James C. Zotalis for their enormous assistance on the executive committee; and to Arliss Reul for her patient and careful secretarial work.

Finally, I would offer my appreciation to all the conference participants who have contributed to this book and acknowledge with a special debt of gratitude the generous grant toward this publication made by the Church Missions Publishing Company, Hartford, Connecticut.

Charles R. Henery

Nashotah House
Nashotah, Wisconsin

Contents

Stepping Westward: A Heavenly Destiny
The Significance of Jackson Kemper

Nelson R. Burr

In thinking of Jackson Kemper, I believe that I have found the right title for this address in William Wordsworth's poem, "Stepping Westward," written in 1807, when Kemper was a youth! The great adventure of our first missionary bishop and his successors seemed to be described in the lines:

And stepping westward seemed to be
A kind of heavenly destiny.

I am not here to give you a very detailed account of Bishop Kemper's life. I come to present a view of his significance in our church's effort to present itself to the new, democratic American people. By the time of his election as missionary bishop in 1835, there was a distinctive American people. A fusion of ethnic groups and cultures was progressing rapidly. Independence from Great Britain already was sixty years old, in a cultural as well as a political sense. And a swelling tide of immigration was bringing new peoples to the American fusion. The Irish were coming. The Germans were coming. The Scandinavians and the Netherlanders were looking westward.

To most of our varied population the Episcopal Church seemed somewhat exotic, a vestige of colonialism—even Toryish! Bishop George W. Doane discovered this in New Jersey as late as the 1830s. Our early bishops all had been born as subjects of Kings George II and III, and obviously were marked with the stamp of English eighteenth-century culture. Their literary education bore the traits of the ancient classics, and of Addison, Steele, Pope and Dr. Samuel Johnson. I believe that we would recognize this fact, if they could live again and converse with us.

Our bishops from the 1820s onward seem somewhat different. They were American-born, and American in education and outlook. And while it may seem like a trifle, the fact that they wore trousers, and regarded a wig as a quaint affectation, really is important. They would be amused that Bishop Abraham Jarvis of Connecticut, a British colonial by birth and culture, was known to refuse to ordain a young man wearing trousers. These are tremendous trifles; they can draw dividing lines.

The new bishops inherited a territorially restricted Church, which clung mostly to the Eastern seaboard—eastern Massachusetts, the shoreline of Narragansett Bay, southwestern Connecticut, the counties around New York City, Philadelphia and the nearby suburbs, the shores of Chesapeake Bay, Tidewater and Piedmont Virginia, and the South Carolina lowlands. Even in the Eastern States it was numerically small in comparison with the so-called "denominations." New Jersey in 1832 had only about 800 communicants. The Church had lost its political privilege: the colonial legal establishments in New York and the South had been discarded by new constitutions and statutes. The Church had become, in fact, one of the many denominations.

To many Episcopalians in the early 1800s the future looked cloudy, even bleak. But westward, look, the land was brightening! Stepping westward had begun, as hordes of New Englanders, including many Episcopalians, streamed into central and northern New York State, northwestern Pennsylvania, and northern Ohio. And far southward, planters and farmers abandoned worn-out land in Virginia, Maryland and the Carolinas to make a fresh start in southern Ohio, Kentucky, Tennessee, Alabama and Mississippi. By 1821 all the area of our country east of the Mississippi River—except Florida, Wisconsin and Michigan—had attained statehood, fourteen years before Kemper was elected.

The Episcopalians who joined the westward trek generally moved as individuals and families. Sometimes an entire parish would move. This fact seized upon my attention on a motor trip across Ohio, when as I passed through Worthington, a northern suburb of Columbus, I crossed Hartford Street and spotted an Episcopal church on one of its corners. The pioneers in this place had departed for Ohio from Worthington, Connecticut, a few miles south of my own home in West Hartford, as a group. And they simply built a New England town on the frontier.

That re-creation of a political and cultural unit suggests that the Church's pioneers before Kemper's time either created or entered an environment not much different from the one they had left. They reproduced the New England town, the Yankee or Southern farm, or the plantation. Thus they laid the groundwork of parishes, which could organize conventions of delegates, which in turn could elect a bishop for consecration—as in Ohio, Kentucky and Tennessee. The Church's episcopate, let us say, grew out of a long familiar setting. That is to say, a reasonably well settled, civilized environment, with churches like those of the Eastern States, also schools, academies and even colleges, town halls, courthouses and general stores.

How different it was for Jackson Kemper and his companions, and their followers! They encountered a vast (and to many fearful) environment, where they couldn't count on finding any of the familiar elements. They were dispatched into the vastness of western America to create them. It seems no exaggeration to say that often they had to start with practically nothing but their own energy, courage and faith. Generally it was that sort of challenge that Kemper and his successors had to take up in the decades after 1835.

What kind of men were they? They were generally and frankly American, without the lingering air of a colonial culture. They were educated in American elementary schools, academies and colleges which stressed general literacy, oratory, Biblical knowledge, in addition to the ancient literary classics. They were American gentlemen scholars, like Kemper with his Columbia College intellectualism. But they were aware that outside of academia there was the common-sense, ruggedly virtuous world of the American "common man." Like Kemper, they respected that man, and he respected them for their courage, daring and manliness. They were not a threat to him, who knew that he had more to fear, sometimes, from his own kind. One thinks of the grave respect with which bishops like Henry B. Whipple, Peter T. Rowe and William H. Hare were regarded.

With such leaders the Episcopal Church broke out of a settled, traditional environment, and stepped westward into an awesome, primitive vastness. It is vividly described in Archibald MacLeish's poem, "American Letter":

It is a strange thing to be an American.
It is strange to live on the high world in the stare
Of the naked sun and the stars as our bones live...
We first inhabit the world. We dwell
On the half earth, on the open curve of a continent...
                                        the prairies
Slide out of dark: in the eddy of clean air
The smoke goes up from the high plains of Wyoming:
The steep Sierras arise: the struck foam
Flames at the wind's heel on the far Pacific.
Already the noon leans to the eastern cliff:
The elms darken the door and the dust-heavy lilacs.

The lilacs in Woodbury, Connecticut, where the Glebe House recalls the election of Samuel Seabury in 1783, before Kemper was born.

Jackson Kemper, and the missionary bishops and priests who succeeded him, did not shrink from "the open curve of a continent," if they survived its first impact upon them, and some did not. One feels that they came to love the rolling prairies, bad lands, dry ranch country, white-toothed mountains with high passes, dark and dripping forests, fiords, glaciers and tundras. The modern New Englander feels awe and wonder when crossing the vastness by train, or by airplane, with the announcer reminding him at long intervals that he is over Minnesota, the Badlands, the Custer Battlefield, the peaks of Idaho, the Columbia River Valley, and Portland at last! For years he remembers the silence of Flint Hills pastures in Kansas, lonely stretches of Oregon coast, miles upon miles of colossal redwood columns, Monterey confronting oceanic vastness. The missionaries knew all these wonders, and many came to love them.

They traversed vastness on horseback, in stagecoaches, on slow trains, by dogsled, and on steamboats that ate up incredible piles of wood stacked on the river banks. After the turn of our century, we see them in those primitive automobiles which are quaint features in the Missionary Society's photograph collection in the archives of the Episcopal Church at Austin, Texas.

The human environment could be just as interesting as the natural, and sometimes as dangerous; likewise the travel. The West was largely a man's world in mining camps, lumber camps, fishing villages, and on vast ranches. When one studies some photos of streets, it is obvious that the board sidewalks and the muddy highways are covered with men. Hastily built towns were often appallingly dirty and smelly and full of diseases. The vast missionary world often was violent and dangerous. Many men were armed, openly or secretly, and there were quarrels, feuds and shootings, such as those chronicled in that classic, *An Album of Gunfighters*, or in the Time-Life books on the West. One senses the dangers in Owen Wister's fiction or Teddy Roosevelt's story of his life on a Dakota ranch. Even a missionary was not always safe. Bishop Charles J. Seghers, the first Roman Catholic prelate in Alaska, was cold-bloodedly murdered by a bad man. Our own Bishop Rowe of Alaska did not escape the hostility of traders and officials.

Into often risky places came the missionaries of the Episcopal Church: to wild mining towns, isolated ranches, Indian villages where they were greeted by yelping dogs and by chiefs of Roman dignity. Sometimes they would be welcomed by a committee of townspeople—mostly women— who might say: "Reverend, we would like to talk with you about the state of religion, or the absence of it, in this place. We have no church, no school. Where can we get help to build them? How long can you stay?" Church, at first, might be a store, an abandoned land office, even a saloon not open on Sunday. On Indian reservations the shelter might be an arbor with a frame of wooden poles and a roof of brush.

Some towns, where we once had churches, have vanished. They are not listed in Rand-McNally's vast index of places. The mind "petered out," or maybe a projected railroad didn't come that way, and that meant doom and desolation.

What does this story mean, the tale of adventure wrought by Kemper's successors, his spiritual children? I think it means that the Episcopal church decided not to be a cultural vestige from the colonial period, and to join with other churches in helping to evangelize and civilize the "open curve of a continent." During several decades after the Revolutionary War, many religious and educational leaders feared that the rapidly advancing Western frontier would sink into a barbarous and irreligious illiteracy. To prevent that they plunged into action on many fronts, and supported a vast number of missionary, Bible, tract and educational associations, with generous help from many devoted lay men and women. Many of the churches, academies and colleges now scattered across the West were founded by that "Benevolent Empire." Our country owes an enormous debt to those patrician, devout and industrious clergymen, and lay men and women. Many of them were related by blood or marriage, or knew each other in business or social affairs. They formed a philanthropic interlocking directorate. And among them were many notable Episcopalians.

The missionary enterprise had a wide and profound effect upon the long-settled churches of the Eastern states. They became accustomed to missionary meetings at General Conventions, and visits of missionaries to parishes and diocesan conventions to seek help. And—like music with the Episcopalian Damrosches—missions discovered the energy of the American woman. In the Woman's Auxiliary she filled mite boxes, and helped to pack innumerable missionary boxes full of clothing, conveniences, toys and many other things, that went in a steady stream to Western and foreign missions. I remember the eager activity when I was in church school and in the choir at St. John's Church, West Hartford. Probably some boxes went to a former rector of my present parish, the Rev. Paul Barbour, who devoted most of his long ministry to the Rosebud Reservation in South Dakota. The spell of the missionary frontier possessed him.

And now we face another frontier, in some ways more dangerous than the West, which Kemper and his spiritual children knew so well. It is not, as theirs was, in a definite region. It is everywhere—in the slums, among the new immigrants, among the poor, the addicts, the neglected, the abused, the lost. It is the frontier of human need and dereliction. It is among the educated and the rich, who sometimes are religiously illiterate and spiritually starved. It is among the leisurely, like the lady in Wallace Stevens' poem, "Sunday Morning." She sits on a sunlit terrace, enjoying coffee and oranges, and meditating on the meaning of Sunday and of that ancient sacrifice of Jesus in the Holy Land. She is comfortable, yet she confesses

But in contentment I still feel
The need of some imperishable bliss.

This bliss was brought to the open curve of a continent when Kemper and his successors ventured to brave its dangers and place upon it the stamp of Christian culture; and which is symbolized by Nashotah House, the memorial to Kemper where we meet today.

The Domestic Missionary Movement in the Episcopal Church in the Nineteenth Century

David L. Holmes

On the surface of things, the Episcopal Church should have achieved a far greater membership than it did in the new south and west. By the nineteenth century Americans were beginning to forget their colonial prejudices against the Church of England. At the same time, the Episcopal Church was in the process of becoming a truly American church. In other ways, too, the time was ripe.

The move into new areas, for example, occurred at almost precisely the time when many Americans were in full revolt against predestinarian Calvinism. Thus Presbyterians and Congregationalists and Reformed should have found the intellectuality and sensibility and theology of the Episcopal Church appealing.

And, in fact, they clearly did. The records indicate that almost one out of every five priests who served from 1800 to 1840 came into the Episcopal Church from a Calvinist background.[1] The same was true of a remarkable number of missionary bishops. If the Episcopal Church had kept statistics for laity, the percentages of converts from Calvinist backgrounds would have been even higher.

Moreover, if Calvinists were in revolt, so, too, as the nineteenth century went on, were Methodists. Many of the Methodists who immigrated directly from England to the American west found the Episcopal Church closer to their background than they did American Methodism with its revivalism and frontier liturgy. In the later years of the nineteenth century, American Methodists themselves became more and more churchly and suspicious of revivalism. Thus it is no surprise that the reports of the western bishops of the Episcopal Church frequently mention the confirmations or ordinations of former Methodists. The same reaction caused clergy and laity from other revivalistic denominations to become Episcopalians.

What else did the Episcopal Church offer that appealed to settlers?

It offered liturgical worship in English. By doing so it attracted Lutherans and Roman Catholics who wished to worship in English, or who were unable to find churches of their own in the new south or west, or both.

In addition, the Episcopal Church offered liturgical worship according to The Book of Common Prayer. In the west as in the American east, people simply read themselves into the Church via The Book of Common Prayer. Others were attracted by the Prayer Book's stately worship, by its extensive use of scripture, or by its involvement of the congregation in worship. Hence settlers who attended Episcopal services out of curiosity were often surprised. "The people . . .were alive with curiosity," a missionary in Arkansas wrote in the 1850s,

> I never heard the responses made with such hearty good-will.
> Having been accustomed, in. . .other denominations, to sit
> as. . .spectators and listeners, they were. . .delighted at the
> idea of being made participants in the worship of God.[2]

An additional appeal lay in Anglicanism's claims of antiquity. In new areas of the new United States, the Episcopal Church could offer settlers the sense that they were part of an ancient tradition—a tradition far older than that of what many High Churchmen loved to call "the sectarians." Thus just as Bishop John Henry Hobart had earlier done in upstate New York, so many Episcopal missionaries in the areas across the mountains took as their platform "The Church—a glorious, old, Apostolic Church." An essentially untold tale is the story of the steady stream of Disciples of Christ clergy and laity—Campbellites involved in a quest for the True Biblical Church—who eventually became Episcopalians for this reason in the south and middle west during the nineteenth century.

Another drawing card for the Church involved the freedoms it permitted its clergy and laity. To be able to dance, go to the theatre, drink alcohol, and participate in other worldly amusements, and still be considered a Christian, attracted many Protestants who were fleeing narrow backgrounds.

Episcopalians could also be Masons—a freedom that appealed to Roman Catholics and to Lutherans who were forbidden Masonic membership. The Church's willingness to tolerate different shades of theological opinion also attracted Christians who desired greater intellectual freedom. The first president of the University of Indiana, for example, seems to have left the Presbyterian for the Episcopal ministry precisely for this reason.[3]

Even the built-in social respectability of the Episcopal Church could have proved an advantage in the domestic missions field. In newly-settled areas of America, Episcopal churches provided ties with English culture and civilization. They furnished a means of escaping from the inevitable crudities of frontier life. Thus many residents of the new south and west felt they had "arrived" when an Episcopal church was established in their town.

Finally, the Church's system of missionary bishops should have provided a major advantage. To be sure, other denominations had missionary superintendents or agents in the field. But only the Episcopal Church had a missionary bishop who was viewed as an apostle and charged with preaching the Gospel to every creature. He had robes and title and prestige. Time and again, when he came into isolated settlements, people felt they had experienced the fullness of the Christian Church.

The Episcopal missionary bishop was a remarkable figure. He travelled and preached more than any of his clergy, and usually he was a better preacher than any of them. Sometimes, as in mining towns and other remote areas, he was the only clergyman people saw from year to year. That he was "The Bishop" usually secured for him wide attention and a respectful congregation.

If the system of missionary bishops should have proved advantageous for the Episcopal Church, so should most of the men who were consecrated to that office during the nineteenth century. Beginning with Kemper's election in 1835, the House of Bishops usually elected missionary bishops only after careful study and after full and frank discussions of the strengths and weaknesses of each possible candidate.

The bishops chose carefully, because they realized that their missionary brethren had to possess special qualities. Vision, an ability to inspire, and a capacity for administration represented only three of the needed qualities. In addition, missionary bishops had to possess what the Victorians would have called "manliness." When a missionary in Missouri declared that "the mountain men with long bodies and shaggy beards admire the Bishop of Missouri so much that they are beginning to consider it manly and respectable to be Christians," he was speaking of precisely the kind of bishop the House of Bishops wanted for the new areas of America.[4]

Hence the bishops elected during the nineteenth century not only for the missionary jurisdictions but also for the western dioceses that remained missionary districts in all but name were younger than those elected for the established dioceses along the eastern seaboard. Sixteen of the first twenty domestic missionary bishops (or eighty percent) were in their thirties or forties when consecrated; two were elected even before their thirtieth birthdays.

Inevitably some missionary bishops proved less effective than others; a few were notably unsuccessful. But the overwhelming majority turned out to be remarkable people. Jackson Kemper, for example, was an unusual combination of gentleness, refinement, scholarship, and toughness. Leonidas Polk was a West Pointer who retained a commanding presence throughout life. Robert Harper Clarkson of Nebraska and Parts Adjacent was described as "a man of singular sweetness of character, rare wisdom, great mellowness of heart, and untiring...labors."[5]

Clarkson himself eulogized George M. Randall of Colorado and Parts Adjacent as "a Bishop who was as truly a martyr to work and to duty for Christ's sake...as any holy man of the past."[6] Daniel S. Tuttle of Montana, Idaho, and Utah not only worked with miners, ranchers, hunters, and fishermen, but endured hardship with a quiet, whimsical humor that caused even notorious outlaws to think of them as *their* bishop. Ethelbert Talbot, who had been raised on a farm, put his familiarity with horses, livestock, and rural people to good use as Missionary Bishop of Wyoming and Idaho. And Peter Trimble Rowe of Alaska seems to have been *sui generis.*

So exceptional was the record of the House of Bishops that a missionary bishop's career usually vindicated his selection even when observers initially believed his election a mistake. In 1866, for example, the House elected William Hobart Hare to the new missionary episcopate of Niobrara.

Raised in the east, Hare was the son of a priest and seminary dean. A contemporary described him as "distinctly a man of fineness and cultivation, one who seemed peculiarly fitted to meet the demands of an intricate and highly organized civilization—in the best sense, a man of the world."[7] Yet the House of Bishops elected him to Niobrara, one of the most isolated of the domestic missionary jurisdictions. "This is the mistake...the Church is always making," one of the bishops reportedly lamented upon leaving that election. "She sets her finest men to her commonest work. She is continually using a razor to split kindling."[8] Hare became perhaps the Episcopal Church's greatest missionary to the Indians.

If the calibre of men who served as missionary bishops should have placed the Episcopal Church at an advantage in the newly-developing states and territories, so should the routines the missionary bishops followed.

Whether in charge of a missionary jurisdiction or a newly independent diocese, the typical Episcopal bishop in the new south or west seems to have remained almost continually in motion. He would sleep in the open or in a tent or in a shared bed. He would ride stages for days and nights on end. He would preach and administer the sacraments in isolated towns. He would organize parishes, establish schools and hospitals, appeal for more clergy, and appeal (often back east) for more funds.

To be sure, the General Convention authorized good salaries for missionary bishops. Usually the bishop and his family lived in a large Victorian home in one of the major towns in his jurisdiction. But once the bishop left home, he lived a life of fatigue, hardship, discomfort, and constant motion.

Kemper, for example, travelled 300,000 miles in the 35 years of his episcopate; for many years he claimed only Christmas to spend with his family. George Washington Freeman, Missionary Bishop of the Southwest, travelled over 12,000 miles in one year. For 13 years, in order to visit 27 churches as well as almost every house and miner's cabin in Montana, Tuttle travelled by horse, ox team, mail wagon, stage coach, and foot. Rowe employed dogsleds, canoes, boats, steamships, railways, automobiles, and finally airplanes to travel over Alaska. Bishop Lemuel H. Wells of Spokane employed ten forms of transportation.

Thus the missionary and western bishops lived lives similar to those of the Methodist circuit riders. They headed a church that possessed many additional advantages. And the Methodists, along with the Baptists, swept much of the new south and west. But the Episcopal Church never did.

Why not? The answer is found in the obstacles to growth that confronted the Episcopal Church in America's new states and territories. The obstacles fell into two categories—those that were not entirely of the Church's making, and those that the Church itself partially or wholly created.

Over what obstacles to church growth did the Episcopal Church have little control? One was that most Americans who left the older areas of the country for the new south or west moved because they were discontent with their economic or social status. And this, of course, meant that relatively few Episcopalians, or even people who were familiar with Episcopal services, went west. As late as the twentieth century, Kansans frequently informed the first Bishop of Western Kansas that they had never before heard of the Protestant Episcopal Church.

That the west (Utah was the only exception) was settled for material reasons formed a second obstacle. Reports from missionaries of all denominations indicate that a general and sometimes scandalous disregard of religion characterized the nineteenth-century west. Granted, the Methodists and other evangelical denominations showed that large numbers of those settlers in reality were open to church membership. And as the west became tamed, that openness increased.

21

But here the Episcopal Church encountered a third built-in obstacle: in the west, as in the east, Episcopal churches tended to attract what was then called "good society." References to doctors, lawyers, public officials, plantation gentry, and leading merchants run through the reports of the Episcopal domestic missionaries. In addition, most Episcopal churches in the new south and west (Minnesota seems to have been the principal exception) rented their pews. They had to rent them to cover expenses, for the Missionary Society could send little financial help.

But the consequences were clear. The average settler who visited an Episcopal church was either uncomfortable with the social strata of its membership, or uncomfortable with Prayer Book services that presupposed literacy and played down emotionalism—or he or she was simply priced out of it.

All denominations experienced the fourth and final obstacle—the mobility of the population. People in the new areas were always settling but never settled. Many Episcopal missionaries, in fact, viewed the floating character of the population as their greatest affliction. For they would painstakingly gather a congregation and painstakingly introduce new communicants to the Episcopal Church only to have them move, and generally move to areas that lacked Episcopal churches, where many would be lost to other denominations or to irreligion.

What obstacles to growth could the Church have done something about? An examination reveals at least five.

First, the Church was late with its missions. The Methodists had circuit riders in place in the new south and west from the 1780s on. The Congregationalists, the Presbyterians, and the Baptists had missionary societies at work from 1800 on. But not until 1821 did the Episcopal Church develop a national missionary strategy.

Created by the General Convention in that year, the Domestic and Foreign Missionary Society (in short form, "the Missionary Society") was initially a voluntary society. Episcopalians concerned with missions voluntarily joined it and paid annual dues. This strategy might have worked in other denominations, but in the Episcopal Church it failed.

The Society's small membership and discouraging results soon forced another strategy.

In 1835, after 14 years of the voluntary approach to missions, the General Convention took the New Testament as its model and declared that missions should be the responsibility of the entire Church. By virtue of their Baptism, it asserted, all Episcopalians were members of the Domestic and Foreign Missionary Society.

The same General Convention also decided on a unique missionary strategy. Prior to 1835, the only way a new state could secure a bishop was for a sufficient number of Episcopalians who lived there to assemble in convention, form a diocese, elect a bishop, and ask the General Convention to consecrate him.

But the General Convention of 1835 decided to carve the new south and west into missionary jurisdictions or districts. It also decided to send missionary bishops into these areas even before any Episcopal work had started in them. Again the model was the New Testament—in this case, the apostle.

Jackson Kemper was the first missionary bishop sent west. That the century was more than one-third over before the tireless and consecrated Kemper took up his work illustrates the obstacles he and the missionary bishops who followed him confronted.

For the results were inevitable. By the time Episcopal missionaries arrived, the best period for evangelization had usually passed. The relatively few settlers who came from Episcopal backgrounds had usually affiliated with other churches. So, too, had settlers from other backgrounds who might have been open to the Anglican interpretation of Christianity. Churches of other denominations dotted the landscape. In the words of Bishop Whipple, tardiness forced the Episcopal Church to be a gleaner instead of a reaper in the new areas of America.[9] Not until after the Civil War, when population began to reach the Plains States, Rockies, and Southwest, did Episcopal missionaries sometimes become the first Christian clergy to visit a town or camp.

Rivalry and tension represent a second reason for the Church's relative lack of success in domestic missions. The conflicts fell into three categories.

First, the needs of local parishes and the needs of national missions conflicted. Pressed by an inability to meet their own needs, some rectors refused to allow agents of the Missionary Society to speak in their churches. Others used money given for missions for parish purposes. All of this hurt the work of the Society, for the General Convention refused to allow the Missionary Society to levy annual assessments for missions. Instead, it compelled the Society to rely upon the parish clergy to be its principal fundraisers.

A related tension occurred between diocesan missions and domestic missions. During the nineteenth century most Episcopal dioceses had their own missions, their own missionary clergy, and their own financial needs for missions. Thus a sense of competing interests emerged where only a common purpose should have existed. This competition caused diocesan bishops to oppose any systematic offering plan for the Missionary Society and, throughout the century, it reduced the money available for planting and nourishing the Episcopal Church in the new areas of America.

The remaining tension—that between church parties—was also the most virulent. A tacit agreement (later regretted by the Evangelicals) placed a majority of High Church members on the Domestic Committee of the Missionary Society; Evangelicals controlled the Foreign Committee. Initially the tensions between the two parties were muted, but they came into the open during the Oxford Movement of the 1830s and 1840s. The tensions caused Evangelicals (who had some of the wealthiest parishes in the Church) not only to reduce or to withhold financial support from domestic missions but also to establish their own, separate domestic missionary society.

A third obstacle involved the size of the jurisdictions the General Convention assigned to missionary bishops. Not only Episcopal polity but common sense dictated that the chief pastor was needed everywhere in his missionary diocese. But the Episcopal Church gave its missionary bishops "dioceses unequalled in extent since the apostles were sent forth to undertake the conversion of the world."[10]

The missionary jurisdictions were huge and unmanageable. At one time or another, Kemper was in charge of all of the territory that now comprises the states of Indiana, Wisconsin, Iowa, Missouri, Minnesota, Nebraska, and Kansas. Initially he intended to spend a week at every parish or mission station in his jurisdiction, but he quickly found that plan a hopeless dream. Polk supervised Arkansas, Mississippi, Louisiana, Alabama, and the Indian Territory. It is "quite impossible for me to do anything effectively over so wide an extent of country," he reported after his first tour of his jurisdiction.[11] He soon left it to become Bishop of Louisiana.

Even when the General Convention divided missionary jurisdictions, the new ones were still enormous. In the 1850s, for example, the General Convention created California and Texas as separate dioceses. One writer pointed out that if Bishop Alexander Gregg of Texas and Bishop William Ingraham Kip of California had divided their dioceses into areas of ten miles square and devoted one week to each, Gregg would have required 52 years and Kip 36 years to complete a single visitation.[12] Even when Texas was divided in the 1870s, each of its new dioceses were still the size of New York, New Jersey, and Pennsylvania combined.

The examples are endless. Joseph C. Talbot (consecrated in 1860 as Missionary Bishop of the Northwest) was given a jurisdiction that embraced what are now the Dakotas, Nebraska, Colorado, Utah, Montana, Wyoming, and Nevada. Styling himself "The Bishop of All Outdoors," Talbot informed the Missionary Society that a bishop living in London could exercise better Episcopal oversight of New York than he could of his own diocese.[13] Talbot's reports of visitations read like this:

... *traveling between three and four thousand miles, up and down the eastern face of the Rocky Mountains through Utah, across the great basin. . .over the Sierra Nevada to San Francisco, thence back to Carson, hither and thither in Nevada, back across the great basin, the Rocky Mountains, and the Plains—in wagons, in stages, in ambulances. . .sleeping in tents, in coaches and by the wayside. . .for weeks, night and day, tossed in most indifferent coaches. . . .*[14]

The enormity of these missionary jurisdictions undercut the Church in the new south and west. "I have never realized, as on this visit," declared a western bishop after his first visitation of his diocese in 1865

the value and importance of a missionary episcopate. A congregation, upon the frontier, few in number and of limited pecuniary resources, far away from the centers of Church sympathy and influence, not informed as to the methods of procuring ministerial supplies, not acquainted with the clergy, and not knowing to whom to apply for assistance, is dependent, in a degree utterly beyond the comprehension of persons in. . .old and populous Dioceses, upon the supervision and aid of the Episcopate.[15]

The size of their dioceses caused missionary bishops to spend more time travelling than they did preaching, encouraging their scattered and often dispirited clergy, inspiring their congregations, or planting new Episcopal churches. The effect on the growth of the Episcopal Church was inevitable.

A continuous shortage of missionaries represented the fourth major obstacle. Episcopal clergy simply did not cross the mountains in either the quantity or quality required.

The laments of the Missionary Society and the bishops about a shortage of priests begin in 1836 and continue throughout the century. Kemper wants 100 clergy immediately; seven years later he has only 31. The Baptists have as many ministers at work in Missouri as the Episcopalians have in all of the trans-Allegheny states combined. No Episcopal clergy can be found for Iowa. Bishop Thomas Fielding Scott cannot persuade a single deacon or priest to accompany him to his new missionary jurisdiction of the Oregon and Washington Territories; when Scott dies, the population of his diocese exceeds 100,000—but he has never had more than 10 clergy to work in it.

"In Montana. . .[not] a single missionary," reads a typical report in *The Spirit of Missions,* "in Arizona no missionary. . . .in Idaho. . .one missionary. . .in Washington one missionary."[16] Years pass between Seward's purchase of Alaska and the arrival of the first Episcopal missionary there. "Cannot the Episcopal Church do anything?" asks an English missionary on the Mackenzie River in 1885. "Cannot it send two or three men to minister to these perishing souls?"[17]

Why so few missionaries? The traditional explanation has been that the Episcopal Church suffered from a shortage of clergy from the Revolution until well into the twentieth century because of its relatively high ordination standards and other, related matters.

But for domestic missions that explanation seems only partially sufficient, precisely because the records indicate that extra clergy were available. Every year Episcopal seminaries graduated new classes. Every year ministers from other denominations converted. Every year rectors and assistants became available for new assignments. Yet the Missionary Society was unable to meet even its modest quotas for domestic missionaries.

Thus a truer explanation may lie in the lack of appeal of domestic missions. In the nineteenth century, as today, most Episcopal clergy came from more or less comfortable backgrounds. As a result, most simply did not wish to go to the new south or west. To them these new areas meant lowered lifestyles, unhealthy conditions, few hospitals and physicians, reduced educational opportunities for children, primitive roads, mobile congregations, few colleagues, uncertain remuneration, and unremitting work.

Morale and debt were problems in the missionary field. Missionaries often quit and came back east. Parish clergy and seminarians knew of these conditions, for they heard the talk or read the missionaries' reports in the Church journals. "It is a fine country to write romances about," wrote one Episcopalian about early Texas, "but it is a very hard one to live in."[18]

What the Church required in the new areas, of course, was a special kind of priest. The Missionary Bishop of North Texas summed up the need when he cried: "Oh, for a man who can ride like a cowboy, pray like a saint, preach like an apostle, and having food and raiment be therewith content."[19] The denominations who had the most success on the frontier—the Methodists and Baptists, the Disciples and Churches of Christ—had such men.

Perhaps the Episcopal Church had them, too. There is some evidence that many of the eastern rectors not only had the right gifts but could have risen to the occasion. The wealthiest parishes in the east, however, almost always picked off gifted young men during their last years of seminary and offered them assistantships or curacies. Thus very few clergy with the right combination of gifts found their way into the domestic mission field.

Where, then, did the missionary bishops get their clergy? Some outstanding priests did come west either because they felt a call, or because they preferred the life of the frontier, or both. Melanchthon Hoyt, perhaps the champion missionary of the west, G.D.B. Miller—who went from Idaho to Japan and then back to Utah—and W. H. Stoy, who served missions throughout the west, would be three examples. Other of the Church's missionaries displayed similar abilities, but the number was always insufficient.

Hence the bishops had to depend upon other sources. Their best clergy tended to come from three sources: eastern clergy who came west upon medical advice; Episcopal chaplains who left the Army but who wanted to stay in the west; or American—or, for that matter, British clergy—who came into the Church from other denominations and who saw that their greatest opportunity lay in the understaffed mission field. The western bishops generally put such clergy to work even before they had been received or ordained.

The worst clergy the bishops received were what Kemper called "poor, crooked sticks"[20]—priests who had failed in the east, seminary graduates who had not received a parish call, or nomadic clergy.

The shortage of missionaries caused the western bishops to realize that they had to raise up a native ministry, for men accustomed to the frontier were best equipped to minister to it. Many of the colleges and seminaries the bishops established in the new states and territories had small enrollments and lasted only a short time. But Nashotah House, Kenyon College, and (until 1968) Bexley Hall stand as examples of what most western bishops hoped to establish.

The lack of missionaries was disastrous for the Episcopal Church. Report after report from the western bishops laments missed opportunities. For lack of harvesters in the field, the Church not only delayed its work in town after town and state after state but also lost countless souls to other denominations.

The fifth, and perhaps the most insurmountable, obstacle confronting Episcopal domestic missions in the nineteenth century was lack of interest. The percentage of Episcopalians who concerned themselves with the missionary work of their Church was perhaps the smallest of any major denomination in the United States.

These pages have already included clear signs of that lack of interest. But many more existed, including no building to house the missionary enterprise until the 1890s, low attendance at the Missionary Society's meetings, and low circulation for its periodical, *The Spirit of Mission*.

Above all, Episcopalians displayed their lack of interest in the financial support they gave to domestic missions. With some notable exceptions, wealthy Episcopalians seem to have spent more for baubles for their children than they did annually on domestic missions. The local parish, followed perhaps by the local diocese, would receive their financial support. But most Episcopalians stopped short when it came to giving money to the domestic mission field.

A classic story tells of Bishop Franklin S. Spalding of Utah on a fund-raising tour of the east. He is invited to speak about the needs of his missions to a dinner party of Park Avenue Episcopalians. "Bishop," says one of his dinner companions before the talk, "there are tens of millions of dollars represented in this room." And afterward, Spalding receives a note of thanks and a check for $25. A lecturer hired to entertain the guests, he said, would have received more.[21]

The century is full of such stories. The Missionary Society is rarely able to meet its lean budgets. Salaries to missionaries are delayed and sometimes a year in arrears. Secretaries of the Domestic Committee wear themselves out trying to raise money, and then resign in frustration. Appeals in church magazines go unanswered.

For the wealthiest Church in America, the statistics are almost unbelievable. As late as the 1860s, fewer than half of Episcopal parishes in America contributed to the Domestic and Foreign Missionary Society. The Society expected so little that it reckoned any year a bumper year in which it received the equivalent of one dollar from each Episcopal communicant. In 1876, when the Episcopal Church spent $4,000 on missionary work in Kansas, that amount was one-seventh of what the Presbyterians spent, one-eighth of what the Congregationalists spent, and one-fifteenth what the Methodists spent. The missionary bishops constantly lament what they are unable to accomplish because they lack the money to pay missionaries and to build and to furnish churches.

Why such a lack of interest in missions? Part of the explanation may lie in the entanglements so many Episcopalians maintained in society, fashion, and luxury. "I come here to find our friends rolling in wealth while missions are dying," a western bishop wrote from New York City in 1870. "You cannot administer the Holy Communion here without seeing on the fingers of those who receive the Body and Blood...wealth enough to make the wilderness blossom as the rose."[22]

Perhaps even more accurate is the assessment that many Episcopalians never developed the kind of burning faith that sees spreading the Gospel as a duty. "I have not met one rich man or woman in Mississippi who seemed willing to suffer the slightest inconvenience for the sake of the Church or its institutions," a Mississippi priest observed in 1894.[23]

But the best answer is probably that many nineteenth-century Episcopalians simply found missions in some way indecorous, ungenteel, and smacking of enthusiasm. "Was there ever a people with so little propagandism about them?" asked an editorial in *The Spirit of Missions* 30 years after Kemper's consecration:

We are too polished and conservative for that...Leave the rough west and the interior to the Methodists and Baptists, and such half-educated sects, and let us refined easterns have this which we are so fitted to enjoy...We...seem to have adopted Talleyrand's famous maxim: 'Above all, no zeal.'[24]

In the midst of all of these obstacles, how were Episcopal churches formed in the new states and territories of the south and west? Occasionally Episcopalians in new settlements would form themselves into a parish and write either to the Missionary Society or to a missionary bishop and ask for a priest. But in most cases the Episcopal missionaries, whether priests or bishops, had to take the initiative and establish churches.

To form a congregation, a missionary (whether bishop or priest) generally began by looking for persons who had been raised as Episcopalians elsewhere. If he was unable to locate any, he paid calls on "respectable and intelligent citizens who might be friendly" to the Church. These or similar class-oriented phrases run through the reports of some missionaries like a refrain, and they inevitably affected mission.

When an Episcopal missionary lacked contacts, he would simply preach in a community, announcing services by posting notices. "The Bishop is coming. Let all turn out and hear the Bishop," went one such notice posted in a new Idaho town by two zealous laymen. "Please leave your guns with the usher."[25] Following such services, the missionary would attempt to form an Episcopal congregation.

Usually the first facilities for Prayer Book worship were makeshift, for missionaries generally had to use whatever buildings they could secure at little or no charge. Homes, schoolhouses, dance halls, Masonic halls, theatres, courtrooms, and saloons—the missionary bishops and priests preached in all of these. Frequently they used one of the abandoned churches that were so common in the nineteenth-century west. Since denominational lines in new settlements were less distinctly drawn than in established communities, Episcopal clergy also held services in churches lent by other denominations. Only the Mormons seem to have opposed Episcopal missionaries with any regularity.

In such settings Episcopal worship was often bare of ornament. Missionaries also tended to omit chants or difficult hymns, singing instead old, familiar hymns. If there was music, a piano or a melodeon provided it. An organ in a borrowed church was a real treat. Except in mining camps, women and children predominated in the congregations.

For all of these reasons the Episcopal missionaries tried to build their own churches as quickly as possible. And this meant that they had to search for money, either locally or back east—for the Missionary Society lacked the funds to assist church construction for many decades. Kemper advocated what he called "cheap and unadorned churches," for he saw too many missionaries and vestries go broke trying to copy eastern churches.[26] The Missionary Society printed designs of log churches in classical and gothic styles designed to accommodate 400 worshippers and to cost less than $1,000. But some of the churches built were much grander.

To establish and nurture parishes, missionaries distributed Bibles, devotional works, Prayer Books, and tracts—especially tracts emphasizing the distinctiveness of the Episcopal Church. They established Sunday Schools quickly, for such schools were a means not only of training children but also of influencing unchurched parents. As a missionary diocese grew, Episcopal schools and hospitals generally followed. Almost unparalleled is James Lloyd Breck's role in establishing such schools both in the middle west and on the Pacific Coast.

Perhaps the least known fact about Episcopal domestic missions is that they used itinerants. All of the missionary bishops, of course, itinerated; in North Dakota Bishop William D. Walker even fitted a 60-foot railroad car as a travelling chapel and took services to remote settlements. But the literature tells of Episcopal circuits all over the west—a circuit of 10 churches in Michigan, of eight in Minnesota, of five in Oregon. In South Dakota, Melanchthon Hoyt itinerated the entire state. In Wisconsin, Breck and his companions formed one of the earliest groups of itinerants.

Thus the appropriate historical question is not: why did the Episcopal Church refuse to follow the example of the Methodists and use circuit riders? For Episcopal missions did have itinerants.

Rather, the right question appears to be: why did only a small percentage of the Episcopal missionaries itinerate? An accurate answer to that important question would probably focus on four considerations: on the stamina and drive of the clergy who chose the mission field; on the lack of an established tradition of itinerancy in Anglicanism; on the desire of Episcopal laity to have full-time rectors; and on the effect itinerancy had not only on salaries but also on family life.

Knowing how effective circuit-riding could be, the western bishops did the best they could to foster it in their jurisdictions, even when every tendency led to a settled ministry.

Some bishops, like Henry B. Whipple of Minnesota, required all rectors to devote at least 10 days of every three months to itinerancy. But such work had small effect when compared to the full-time circuit-riding that helped Methodism sweep the new south and west.

And so this brief survey of Episcopal domestic missions in the nineteenth century comes to an end. The story is not one of Anglican triumphalism. The Episcopal Church failed to become a major presence in most parts of the deep south and west; in most of the areas settled after the American Revolution, it remained an ecclesiastical exotic. On the whole, with the exception of its remarkable achievements among the Indians, it failed to touch permanently the plain-folk of the new areas. It should have; it could have. Histori-cally, the Episcopal Church could claim to be the mother church of all British Protestants. Liturgically, it was close to Lutheranism and to Roman Catholicism.

But the Church came in with too little, too late—with too few men, too little money, too little administrative support, too little spirit. Inevitably the mind is drawn to measures that might have helped overcome these obstacles: a greater use of the laity, a greater openness to emotion, farmer-priests.

Yet in the end a reader of the Church's missionary history comes back to the realization that domestic missions sim-ply had a low priority for Episcopalians in the nineteenth century. And so the Church reaped what it sowed, and the story of its domestic missionary movement remains more frustrating than inspiring.

Still, mere historical negatives, while ample and accurate, seem insufficient to describe the domestic missionary move-ment of the Episcopal Church. For it is impossible to read about Episcopal missions without being struck by the mis-sionary and western bishops. There is something about men like Kemper, Tuttle, Whipple, Hare, Talbot, Spalding and the others that grips the mind and stirs the imagination. In a tradition that began across the Atlantic with bewigged and gaitered Lord Bishops, these bishops were a new American breed—going into saloons to seek out potential parishion-ers, riding in stages or on horses for days, sleeping and cooking in the open, posting notices of services in mountain hamlets that had never seen a minister of Jesus Christ, arriving for worship covered with dust, going into what they called the new and unoccupied territories to make disciples and to baptize.

"I dare not tell you," said Whipple in his sermon at Clarkson's consecration in 1865

that a Bishop's life is a way of roses. You will miss the strength and comfort of the ties which bind a parish priest to his flock. You will feel like a man who has drifted out to an unknown sea, where there is no help but to cry to God our father. You will be misunderstood. You will encounter prejudice. Your godly discipline may provoke prejudice. Your godly discipline may provoke hatred. Your own sons may stand aloof. You may be weary with deferred hope. You may be faint with the sight of unoccupied fields. There will be times when you would gladly exchange your bishopric for the humblest parish in the land—if it were not that he who taketh the plow and looketh back is not worthy of the kingdom of God.

And yet with all which will make the heart ache and the feet bleed, you will find this a holy, a happy, and a blessed life. I know of no joy like the privilege of being the herald of Christ to new and unoccupied fields.[27]

End Notes

[1]William W. Manross, *The Episcopal Church in the United States, 1800-1840* (New York: Columbia University Press, 1938), 70-71.

[2]*The Spirit of Missions,* 17 (1852), 110 (hereafter cited *SOM*). Cf. William Paret, *Reminiscences* (Philadelphia: Geo. W. Jacobs & Co., 1911), 18.

[3]William B. Sprague, *Annals of the American Pulpit,* 9 vols. (New York: Robert Carter and Bros., 1857-69), 5, 781, 787.

[4]*Home and Abroad* 7, (1876), 43.

[5]William J. Barnds, *The Episcopal Church in Nebraska: A Centennial History* (Omaha: Omaha Printing Co., 1970), 10.

[6]Allen D. Breck, *The Episcopal Church in Colorado* (Denver: Big Mountain Press, 1963), 28, 64-65. Cf. Breck, "The Episcopal Church in Colorado: 1857-1979," *The Colorado Episcopalian,* September 29, 1979, 4.

[7]*SOM*, 74 (1901), 919.

[8]*SOM*, 74 (1909), 920.

[9]*SOM*, 29 (1864), 267.

[10]William Stevens Perry, ed., *The History of the American Episcopal Church, 1587-1883*, 2 vols. (Boston: James R. Osgood and Co., 1885), 2, 248.

[11]William M. Polk, *Leonidas Polk: Bishop and General*, 2 vols. (New York: Longman, Green and Co., 1893), 1:143.

[12]Julia C. Emery, *A Century of Endeavor, 1821-1921: A Record of the First Hundred Years of the Domestic and Foreign Missionary Society...* (New York: The Department of Missions, 1921), 164-165.

[13]*SOM*, 30 (1865), 491. Cf. Colin B. Goodykoontz, *Home Missions on the American Frontier* (Caldwell, Idaho: The Caxton Printers, 1939), 323-324.

[14]*SOM*, 29 (1864), 1.

[15]Blanche M. Taylor, *Plenteous Harvest: The Episcopal Church in Kansas, 1837-1972* (Topeka: Josten, 1973), 81-82.

[16]*SOM*, 30 (1865), 458-461.

[17]Emery, 203-204.

[18]*SOM*, 17 (1852), 49.

[19]*SOM*, 49 (1884), 562.

[20]Greenough White, *An Apostle of the Western Church* (New York: Thos. Whittaker, 1900), 137.

[21]Henry Knox Sherrill, *Among Friends*, (Boston: Little, Brown & Co., 1962), 41.

[22]*SOM*, 35 (1870), 635.

[23]*The Southern Churchman*, 59 (February 8, 1894), 4.

[24]*SOM*, 30 (1865), 43.

[25]Ethelbert Talbot, *My People of the Plains* (New York: Harper & Bros., 1906), 87-88.

[26]Perry, 2, 257, 254.

[27]Barnds, 66.

Lay Workers in the Vineyard:
Insights from the Domestic Committee
of the Episcopal Church
During Bishop Kemper's Episcopate

V. Nelle Bellamy

On September 25, 1835, Jackson Kemper was consecrated the first missionary bishop for the Episcopal Church in the United States of America. He was sent to the old Northwest Territory in a period when the new nation was expanding and moving relentlessly westward across this continent. The Episcopal Church thus sought to send the Church as she had received it to the hardy pioneers. She sent a bishop.

The instrument for this missionary enterprise was the Domestic Committee of the Domestic and Foreign Missionary Society of the Episcopal Church. The society began as a volunteer organization in the church in the 1820s. This formation of a society as the agent for missionary activity was not peculiar to the Church in the new nation. The Church of England had, and has to this day, two very distinguished societies which sent and sends missionaries throughout the world. The Society for the Propagation of the Gospel in Foreign Parts was founded in 1701 and the Church Missionary Society in 1799. Unlike the English societies, the Domestic and Foreign Missionary Society became an integral part of the Episcopal Church and in 1835 included all members. A resolution in the report of the Committee on the Domestic and Foreign Missionary Society to the General Convention recommended that the minister of each congregation "make known to the members of his congregation that they are regarded by the constitution of the Domestic and Foreign Missionary Society as members of the same, and are requested to contribute periodically to its funds."[1] The Domestic and Foreign Missionary Society did its work through the Foreign Committee for countries outside the United States and through the Domestic Committee for work within the United States. There were annual and triennial meetings of the Society with reports from the committees and reports from the bishops who were sent out by the committees. The minutes and reports of the Domestic and Foreign Missionary Society and its committees are in the archives of the Episcopal Church and accessible to scholars and researchers.

My initial purpose in this paper was to discern the role of women workers in the missionary outreach of the Domestic Committee. I arbitrarily chose the years of Bishop Kemper's missionary episcopate as an appropriate time span. Jackson Kemper was consecrated in 1835 and resigned in 1859 on the eve of the Civil War to work only in Wisconsin. Then I set out to examine the minutes and reports of the Domestic Committee for those 25 years of missionary activity, 1835-1859. Bishop Kemper was in Missouri, Indiana, Wisconsin, Iowa, Minnesota, Nebraska, Kansas and the Indian Territory at various times. I also consulted the reports of Bishop George W. Freeman who was appointed missionary bishop for Arkansas in 1844 and later had jurisdiction of the Southwest; Bishop James H. Otey who was elected in Tennessee in 1833; and Bishop William Ingraham Kip who was elected by the House of Bishops for California in 1853. Then I moved from the contributions of women workers to those of laymen at that time; there were laymen involved. The basic question became, "What do these records of the Domestic Committee between 1835 and 1859 reveal about the contributions of lay workers, women and men, to the missionary movement of the Episcopal Church?" Related to that question was a second one, "How do *these* lay contributions from the first half of the nineteenth century compare with lay contributions in this second half of the twentieth century?" Both women and men had responsible lay tasks in the western Church during the Kemper episcopate. Who were they, where were they located and what tasks were they assigned?

Where were women workers involved in this missionary enterprise and in what capacity? Within the annual reports for the Domestic Committee there are names of a small number of women who were teachers at the Green Bay Mission and at Duck Creek, Oneida County, in Wisconsin. From 1835-1842, eight years, the names of Miss Susan Crawford and Miss Senah Crawford are in the reports from Green Bay.[2] In 1841 there are references to their students who were taught to weave and sew as well as learn basic academic skills.[3] The records tell us little about these women and there is only one letter in the archives from either of them; there is one from Miss Senah Crawford to the Rev. Drs. James Milnor and Kemper from Green Bay in 1834.[4] She is describing the children in the school and their mixed racial origins. In 1836 there is also a Mrs. Brown; she is the wife of the Rev. Daniel E. Brown, the superintendent. She is there in 1837 and 1838. The Rev. Mr. Brown and Mrs. Brown resigned from Green Bay in 1839.[5] The names of two women are in the reports about Duck Creek. A Miss S. A. Williams was there in 1838, 1839 and 1840. In 1841 she had retired because of ill health. In 1842 Miss Williams returned.[6] The woman worker who was singled out for praise by Bishop Kemper was the wife of the superintendent, the Rev. Soloman Davis. Her name appears in the early reports; Bishop Kemper refers to her in 1843 and 1846; she probably retired with her husband. The Domestic Committee reports his resignation in 1848.[7] In Bishop Kemper's report for 1843 he writes of Mrs. Davis' great dedication.

The excellent wife of Mr. Davis, acts toward the congregation as a primitive deaconess. Under her husband she is friend and spiritual advisor of the women. They hail her as mother, and she bears, after a long and intimate acquaintance with them, this delightful evidence to their conduct: "I do not," said she with emphasis and much earnestness, "I do not believe that there is an equal number of christian women in our country, who are more circumspect in all their work and conversation, than are these Oneida females."

In 1846, Bishop Kemper pays further tribute to her
who had devoted the best years of her life to the most patient and successful instruction in Scripture truths of the benighted and child-like minds of the female members of the congregation.

Laymen were also employed in these early years. They are named in the reports for Green Bay and Duck Creek. In 1836 two men are listed, Mr. J. G. Knapp and Mr. S. B. Sherwood, for Green Bay.[8] In 1838 there is a Mr. E. Sherwood; there is a Mr. Edson Sherwood listed in 1839 as a farmer; he was there through 1842.[9] At Duck Creek Mr. S. B. Sherwood was listed as a schoolmaster in 1837. He was there in 1838.[10] An Aristogenes Nimham is listed as interpreter in 1837.[11]

One finds the names of women and men in the early reports in the 1830s; later the reports refer to laymen, teachers and interpreters, but do not often give names. A chart of missionary work for 1844 lists an interpreter and a teacher at Duck Creek.[12] The reports of the Domestic Committee from 1847-1850 note that there are three laymen in the pay of the department; and further lists a teacher and an interpreter for Duck Creek.[13] In 1851 there are only two laymen "connected with the Domestic Missionary department" and a teacher and interpreter listed for Duck Creek.[14] After 1851 there are no lay people listed as connected with the Domestic Committee.

The records of the Domestic Committee reveal little personal data about these lay workers. The historian would certainly welcome biographical data about the Misses Crawford. Why were they at Green Bay for those years? What was the quality of their lives? Were they lonely? Were they happy? Or are these twentieth century questions? It is easier to understand how Mrs. Davis arrived at Duck Creek. She came with her husband. Detailed biographical data, while interesting, is not necessary for the subject of this paper. This data does reveal that there were some "professional" type lay workers employed through the Domestic Committee's work, although they are not listed with the appointed missionaries. They taught domestic skills and basic educational ones, were interpreters and managed the farms. They had, apparently, very specific areas of endeavor. They do not appear to be "volunteers" as we think of volunteers in the Church today.

Although there were these few "professional" type lay workers, one must not be deceived. The Church in Bishop Kemper's episcopate was largely a clerical one in its professional life. It was a Church of the clergy in terms of professional status. This is very clearly illustrated in a comment in Bishop Freeman's report in 1856. He writes about a school in Arkansas which had temporarily been left in the care of a layman.

*The school, to be sure, is going on, under the direction of
R. W. Macklin, a worthy lay member of the Church; but it
requires, as Mr. M. himself says, a clergyman of standing,
and of reputation as an instructor of youth, at its head, to
give it character and efficiency.*[15]

The contributions of laymen and laywomen in the missionary world of the Episcopal Church at the time of Bishop
Kemper were seen for the most part in their volunteer
activities in the Church. These activities are a part of the
ministry given through baptism to all of us. This was especially true of women. Even in those days they were involved
in raising money for various causes. There were references
to fairs and sewing circles. They come to the attention of the
Domestic Committee with these activities. The Rev. Richard
F. Cadle in a report in 1836 noted that "the ladies of the
Benevolent Society of the Parish" provided $1,700 toward a
building project.[16] They had organized a fair in September
of that year. Since the estimated cost of the church building
was $3,000, they did well indeed. Other examples of this kind
abound. In 1841 the ladies of Trinity Church, Danville, Kentucky, raised $100 for a bell for the church.[17] Bishop Kemper
in his report for 1850 praised the ladies at Madison, Wisconsin, who helped secure a lot for the church.[18] Women were
also recognized by the Domestic Committee as they organized and taught in church schools. Bishop Freeman in
his 1853 annual report praised a member of a church in
Fayetteville.

*The church at Fayetteville, Arkansas has sustained a great
loss in the death of Mrs. Dean, a prominent member of the
Congregation, and a truly pious and devoted churchwoman.
Perhaps no individual of the parish has contributed more to
the building up of the congregation, and to the extending of
the knowledge of truth as it is held and taught in the Church,
or done more, in acts of beneficence and christian charity,
to illustrate the christian character than that most excellent
lady. Long will her loss be mourned.*[19]

There is also evidence of the activities of laymen in the
churches. The references to lay readers are numerous. Here
are some random examples. Bishop Kemper in 1842 reports
that he has licensed five lay readers;[20] in 1849 he reports that

he licensed ten persons, three of whom were candidates.[21] In 1843 Bishop Otey names a Dr. Styles as a lay reader.[22] In 1851 Bishop Freeman notes the faithfulness of a Mr. W. L. Lastwell, a lay reader.[23] Bishop Kip writes of licensing two lay readers in 1855 who were United States Army officers.[24] The names of laymen also appear in the Domestic Committee reports as lay members of the committee. They were quite influential in this role.

Finally one must not overlook the financial contributions, the legacies, given to the Domestic Committee by committed laymen and laywomen. These people are listed by name in the minutes of the Committee with the amount given to the Church's work.[25]

This compilation of data found in the Proceedings of the Domestic Committee of the Domestic and Foreign Missionary Society, 1835-1859, provides insights for Bishop Kemper's time and for ours. It indicates that there were lay workers in the missionary expansion of the Church westward in Bishop Kemper's episcopate but not a large number. Although we may not have had names and places, statistics and quotations at our immediate command, we have certainly known that the Church at that time was largely a clerical one with few opportunities for what we might today call lay professional roles. This Church seems to have understood the lay ministries to which we are all called by virtue of our baptisms, and also the possibility, although limited, of professional lay positions in the Church. As one looks back one hundred and fifty years to the structure of Bishop Kemper's Church it seems to be a fairly well-ordered one. There was a place for all to participate and the areas of contribution were well-defined. The bishop was selected and sent forth through the General Convention and the Domestic Committee. The Rt. Rev. Jackson Kemper travelled about over Indiana, Missouri, Wisconsin, Iowa, Nebraska, Kansas and Minnesota. The Indian Territory was a part of this. He visited mission stations and, as dioceses developed, parishes were established. In the mission stations one finds an appointed, ordained male clergyperson in charge. He was the appointed missionary. Working with him one might find assistants who were male or female teachers, male or female interpreters, male lay readers, and possibly an assistant in charge of farming. At least this is the picture in Kemper's early episcopate. The picture is not as obvious in the later years. In parishes there would be a clergyman, lay readers and the various women's groups. Women's organizations seem to have existed in mission stations also. If lay people sought to participate in a congregation or mission station, there were certain recognized positions that were open to them. If the Misses Crawford at Green Bay wanted to be superintendents of the school we do not know about it. If they dreamed of ordination to the priesthood there is no evidence of it. They taught the Indian girls to sew and weave. Had they longed for the priestly status they would not have admitted it to Bishop Kemper and probably not to themselves. It was not an option. The priorities of leadership seem to have been first, the bishop, then appointed missionaries and ordained clergy in congregations, lay readers and teachers, lay men and women in the congregations. Although women volunteers were raising money for the fabric of the churches as well as for the programs and were thereby exercising a type of clout and responsibility, they were not considered leaders in the structure.

Does this structure continue in the Episcopal Church in the later part of the twentieth century? Do we find acceptable positions for lay workers; if so, what responsibilities may they undertake? The Church has obviously changed during the past one hundred and fifty years and new areas of participation for lay workers have emerged. You may or may not think that this more recent situation is desirable or even theologically permissible. I must admit that as a professional lay person in this church there are times when the so-called "good old days" in which the parish priest was always right and Father "knew best" seem to have been an easier way of life. But that is nostalgic and I do not really want to turn the clock back.

In our times the ordination of women to the diaconate and the priesthood has provided a clerical vocation for women which was not a possibility in the first half of the nineteenth century. Today women workers may be ordained or lay. The action of General Convention in 1970 approved the ordination of women to the diaconate and in 1976 the ordination to the priesthood. The vote in the House of Deputies in 1976 was not a strong one and in the House of Bishops it was understood that those bishops who in conscience could not ordain women would not be required to do so. All of this was over ten years ago and the heartache and turmoil have not subsided. Women are not ordained in a number of dioceses; in others the bishops are willing to ordain but parishes will not accept women priests. The heartache lies with those who cannot accept, for traditional or theological reasons, the ordination of women as well as with those who have been ordained and are unable to find jobs in this Church. An article in the *New York Times*[26] about three years ago concerning the role of women clergy in mainline protestant churches in the United States cited the Episcopal Church as the one that had the most difficulty in accepting women clergy. Those of us who have followed the debates on the ordination of women in the Church of England pray that the recent Synod action to move toward the ordination of women to the diaconate will not bring about a split in that part of the Anglican Communion. In this Episcopal Church USA the option of priesthood as a vocation for women is a part of our lives whether we accept it theologically or reject it. We must each in our own way live with our consciences, our emotions and the reality of the situation. My basic concern in this paper does not lie with the opening of the priesthood to women and I do not intend to offer an apologia for or against it. My remarks are descriptive.

The Episcopal Church is returning today as she has been wont to do from time to time to an emphasis on lay ministries. The rhetoric is evangelistic and calls lay people to take their rightful places in the ministry of the Church. And I find nothing to fault in this. We are all given ministries through our baptism into the Body of Christ, His Church. And yet the Church is not careful with her language as she refers to lay ministries; she fails to distinguish between that all-encompassing ministry of the laity that is given through baptism and a more "professional" lay ministry that might be an option for non-clerical members of the Church. Lay volunteers work in our churches especially in the parishes and they are valuable and necessary in the ongoing life of the Church. They are lay readers, members of the altar guild, teachers in church schools, parish visitors, members of the vestry and hold other positions. These are lay workers as they minister in the kingdom. They are volunteers, if you will. Then there are "professional workers." As lay workers they have positions in the Church and see them as a vocation. They receive salaries and the usual benefits commensurate with their jobs. A reasonable amount of responsibility is required.

In Bishop Kemper's Church there were lay workers who were "volunteers" and there were lay workers who were "professionals." The largest numbers were, as is to be expected, the volunteers. There were those gracious and generous folk who gave of their wealth to the Church. These were men and women, and their names are often entered in the minutes of the Domestic Committee. Many able men served on the Domestic Committee and participated in the decision-making process. The reports of the bishops include references to lay readers, men at that time, whom they had licensed. The references to ladies' organizations are numerous. The groups of women raised money to maintain the fabric of their churches or to build new ones. They taught in the Sunday schools. They baked goodies and sold them in local fairs. These women in their churches were doing for the Church those domestic-type activities that were expected of them in the culture in which they lived. These were not "professional" positions; these activities were those of volunteers.

According to the reports of the Domestic Committee there were some "professional" lay workers in the first part of the nineteenth century. The teachers listed for the Indian missions of Green Bay and Duck Creek were certainly "professionals." Senah and Susan Crawford appear in the reports for over six years. They taught sewing, weaving and basic academic skills. The farmer, Mr. Edson Sherwood, was listed as an assistant for Green Bay. There are references to teachers and interpreters. All of these positions required more than volunteer responsibilities. Also there are notations about those "employed" by the Domestic Committee in the reports.

44

These lay vocations were not numerous and they were in keeping with the expectations of the culture. Women could teach domestic skills and reading and writing. They were the experts in domestic skills. It seems, then, that there is nothing terribly unusual in these appointments.

What then of "professional" lay positions in the Episcopal Church in the 1980s? Bishop Kemper's era employed only a few such workers and they did very much what they would have done in the secular culture. This was especially true of women's vocations. What professional jobs are open for lay people in the Church today? Many questions arise. In an age of high technology and the availability of university educations, does the Episcopal Church take seriously the fact that there may be highly specialized lay positions that do not require clerical credentials? And if we do take account of this situation do we view such professions as secondary in relation to the priestly profession? Might it not be the case that there would be fewer vocations to the priesthood among women if there were positions of equal status for lay people? Is not the present structure of clergy and laity fostered by the clergy? If there are able persons in a parish who are devoted and committed laborers in the Church, are they not often approached by the clergy and encouraged to move on to ordination?

I must stop here for clarification. These questions do not in any way presume to demean the traditional status of the priestly vocation in the Church. Ours is a catholic tradition and experience with nurturing sacraments and the pastoral care of the priests; I want therefore to affirm the priestly office and its centrality in the Church. I also want to affirm, however, the possibility of professional lay vocations that might be a vital and integral part of the Church. Cannot the priestly office be assisted by a professional lay office? I would hope so. And this possibility and reality are both more evident in the Church today than at any time in its history. There are lay professors in our seminaries. Recently the Board of Theological Education had a lay woman director and a very able one she was. One of the units of the national Church Center has a layman as its head. The Seminary of the Southwest has a two-headed administration: there is the dean who is a priest and recently we have hired a provost who is a layman. The Diocese of Panama has a large number of lay people in the diocesan office. There are many other examples. And yet it seems that the Church continues to have difficulty in discerning the appropriate place for professional lay vocations in a tradition that has emphasized the priestly vocation.

If we seek a kind of shared leadership in the Church by lay workers, we then must ask the practical question, "What responsibilities should such persons have?" Not priestly. Not sacramental. Those are given through ordination. There are, though, other tasks which lay people might assume and thereby leave the priests free to fulfill their very demanding office. At least I think so. The difficulty seems to be that we have few if any models, or so we think. Here is a case. Recently a woman seminarian called me to task when she said, "I overheard you say that women need not be ordained to have a job in the Church. Can you tell me what those non-clerical jobs are?" I was very little help in the practical application of my statements. I could think of very few lay positions in the Church that were what might be called professional and carried with them a reasonable salary and appropriate benefits.

Today I am unable to present many practical applications in my apologia for professional lay positions in the Church. Two models come to mind: one modern and one fourth century. In Scotland I recently met a laywoman who is a member of a parish leadership team which includes lay and ordained people. She has a theological degree from Durham University in England and is licensed by the ordinary for the parish in which her team works. She has a keen sense of her lay vocation and her contribution to her parish. This situation might present insight for us. I asked if she would press for ordination if that were possible in the Episcopal Church in Scotland. She affirmed again that her vocation was a lay one. The second model is one from the Church in Jerusalem in the fourth century. The occasion was the presentation of catechumens to the bishop as he received them in his cathedral. The bishop's procession entred: "First the vowed virgins and widows, deacons, presbyters, and, last, the bishop. The bishop took his throne, and the presbyters their seats on either side. The rest of the procession took positions standing behind the presbyters."[27] Who were these "vowed virgins and widows"? They were not of ordained clergy. They were a type of lay order for women in the early Church. I do not want to draw the practical possibilities of this model; but I leave it with you for your consideration.

With these two models, one modern and the other ancient, I would add a quotation from a modern English author. Sara Maitland is the wife of a priest in the Church of England. She has written an interesting book entitled, *A Map of the New Country: Women and Christianity.* She does not advocate the ordination of women to the priesthood and says quite clearly that for ecumenical reasons she cannot do this. She does explore lay participation in the Church. In her book she refers to a sermon by the Rev. Carter Heyward, whose text had been, "The harvest is plentiful but the laborers are few; pray therefore the Lord of the harvest to send out laborers into his harvest." Ms. Maitland then comments that the Rev. Ms. Heyward had "interpreted 'laborers' as *priests*— Christians for whom 'the commitment to priesthood is central to their vocation, their profession, their life.'" Ms. Maitland, then, concludes

As a lay person I rather resent the implication that God requires only priestly labourers for the harvest.[28]

Sarah Maitland clearly discerns the situation in the Episcopal Church and in the Church of England today where the move for ordination of women has overshadowed the possibilities of types of non-ordained vocations in both Churches.

In closing, we return to Bishop Kemper's Church. There were lay workers in that Church as it moved across this continent. There was little expectation for extensive lay participation at the professional level; the lay participation was therefore largely that of committed volunteers. And yet there were "professional" lay workers and their tasks were those that the culture recognized as appropriate. This is not the case in the Episcopal Church today; the culture provides the possibility of many professional positions for lay people. Many lay folks today are highly educated and possess skills needed in the Church. The professional workers in the first half of the nineteenth century were often teachers of domestic skills and basic tools for reading and writing. Surely today's Church can move beyond this. Although we have a highly trained laity, there is little professional opportunity for them in the Church. It appears this way, but it need not be thus. No longer need the priest be a "Renaissance Man" fulfilling all leadership roles. Lay vocations that assist the priest in some non-priestly tasks permit more time for those responsibilities that are peculiarly given through ordination. It is this professional lay ministry that I want to leave with you for your consideration.

As a final statement, it seems appropriate to remark that Bishop Kemper's Church may have called upon lay talents to the extent that the culture permitted. In the Church today we do not do as well in utilizing the possibilities for lay workers. The culture would provide far more opportunities than the Church presently accepts.

End Notes

[1]*Journal of the Proceedings of the Bishops, Clergy, and Laity, of the Protestant Episcopal Church in the United States of America in A General Convention*. . . . (New York: Protestant Episcopal Press, 1835), 123. A newly amended Constitution of the Domestic and Foreign Missionary Society was adopted by the House of Bishops and House of Deputies. Article II read, "The Society shall be considered as comprehending all persons who are members of this Church." Ibid., 99, 129.

[2]The reports, minutes and other data are found in the annual *Proceedings* of the Society from 1835 through 1858. *Proceedings of the Domestic and Foreign Society of the Protestant Episcopal Church . . . 1835.* (Philadelphia: Wm. Stavely, 1835). *Proceedings. . .* (New-York: Protestant Episcopal Press, 1836). *Proceedings. . .* (New-York: W. Osborn, 1837). Osborn printed the *Proceedings for* 1838 and 1839. *Proceedings. . .* (New-York: Missionary Rooms, 1840). *Proceedings* for 1841, 1842 and 1843 were printed in Missionary Rooms. *Proceedings. . .* (New-York: Daniel Dana, Jr., 1844). *Proceedings. . .*, 1845 (no title page). *Proceedings. . .*, 1846 (no title page). *Proceedings. . .* (New-York: Daniel Dana, Jr., 1847). *Proceedings* for 1849, 1850, 1851, 1852, 1854, 1855, 1856, 1857, 1858 were printed by Dana. *Proceedings* for 1848 and 1853 have no title page.

These *Proceedings* hereafter cited "P," followed by date and page. The references to Miss Susan Crawford and Miss Senah Crawford are found in: P,1835,27; P,1836,30; P,1837,35; P,1838,31; P,1839,23; P,1840,21; P,1841,25;

P,1842,29. The reference in 1835 has Sarah Crawford rather than Senah Crawford. I cannot explain this.

[3]P,1841,85.

[4]Senah Crawford to the Rev. Drs. Milnor and Kemper, 21 July 1834, in the Domestic and Foreign Missionary Society Records: Domestic Committee Records, RG 50-4, Archives of the Episcopal Church, Austin, Texas.

[5]P,1836,30; P,1837,35; P,1838,31; P,1839,24-25.

[6]P,1839,33; P,1839,28; P,1840,22; P,1841,26; P,1842,30. In 1840 she is listed as S. M. Williams; I assume this is a printing error since there is no reference to a new person.

[7]P,1838,33; P,1839,28; P,1840,22; P,1841,26; P,1842,30; P,1843,81; P,1846,60; P,1848,211.

[8]P,1836,30.

[9]P,1838,31; P,1839,23-25; P,1840,21; P,1841,25; P,1842,29.

[10]P,1837,38; P,1838,33.

[11]P,1837,38.

[12]P,1844,62.

[13]P,1847,20,273; P,1848,206,281; P,1849,19,97; P,1850,26,87.

[14]P,1851,15,102.

[15]P,1856,91.

[16]P,1836,33-34.

[17]P,1841,93.

[18]P,1850,62.

[19]P,1853,494.

[20]P,1842,39.

[21]P,1849,52.

[22]P,1843,88.   [23]P,1851,85.   [24]P,1855,140.

[25]See, for example: P,1844,25,32; P,1845,235; P,1846,27; P,1847,22.

[26]Charles Austin, "Women Ministers Feel Responsibility of Dual Role," *New York Times*, 10 April 1983.

[27]Cyril of Jerusalem, "The Catechetical Lectures," ed. William Telfer, in *The Library of Christian Classics*, vol. 4 (London: SCM Press, Ltd, 1955), 64, n. 1.

[28]Sara Maitland, *A Map of the New Country: Women and Christianity* (London: Routledge and Kegan Paul, 1983), 121.

Images of Mission in
the Episcopal Church

W. Roland Foster

I would like to begin by emphasizing the importance of
the word "images" in my title. I have found that a valuable
way of understanding people of the past (or the present, for
that matter) is to ask what images they use—often almost
unconsciously, without thinking about them. And I would
like to stretch the word "images" to include words which
we cannot picture, but which have the quality and power
of images. Words like "catholic" or "democracy" or "com-
munism" carry power and force far beyond their dictionary
meaning.

When I was here at Nashotah House I first began to be
interested in images of identity for this Church. What were
the images by which this Church distinguished itself, which
gave it meaning and self-consciousness? Later I started to
ask questions about mission, and I discovered that the relationship between "mission" and "identity" was almost a
chicken and egg one. Who we think we are shapes profoundly what we do on mission, and our mission in turn
reshapes the thinking of who we are.

Among the most powerful of those images is all that is implied by the word "establishment." It is hard for Americans,
who breathe a denominational air, to get some feel for the
inner character of an established church, so let me begin by
underscoring and contrasting our inheritance as an English
establishment with the American climate.

In the first place, history is important for an established
church. Its institutions and confessions were shaped by that
history, and its important, authoritative figures are known
in that history. Names like Richard Hooker and Lancelot
Andrewes carried weight even in eighteenth century
England. In America, however, there was no national his-

tory to appeal to, only denominational history; and in 1800 American denominations had little of that! So, American denominations had to bypass history and appeal solely to Holy Scripture, and more especially to the New Testament. They must claim to be shaped by the New Testament and faithful to the New Testament alone.

Or again, think of the local church. In Bemerton near Salisbury Cathedral, George Herbert ministered to a congregation that included everyone in Bemerton. Village and church were identical. In New London, Connecticut, Samuel Seabury ministered to a tiny handful of the people of that port, all of whom had joined voluntarily and who might choose to leave if they were not happy. The denomination was voluntaristic in a way the established church could never be. An established church has parishes. A denomination has congregations.

Or look again at the role of a minister or a priest. In eighteenth century England the parish priest was (ideally at least) a pastor to all the people of the village and a civil servant for the government. He baptized everyone in the village, married and buried them all. He kept his own garden, often ran a small school, conducted services and preached mediocre sermons to a packed and often ancient parish church. Sometimes he read a lot, and usually he received funds from endowments that went back for centuries. But the American minister or priest had a different assignment. His scope was the congregation, not the village. He had to build up his flock, evangelize new members, keep the congregation thriving, preach stirring sermons, and try to get a living income from the faithful. He seldom had time to read.

Now think about mission. The differences of identity between an established church and a denomination profoundly change their understanding of mission. An established church has little concern for evangelism. All members of the nation are automatically members of the church. There is no competition for members since there are no competitors, simply the established church. Mission means making the gospel more relevant to daily and national life, ministering to the hurt, the newly born, the dying. Archbishop William

Laud saw the Stuart Church as the "conscience of the nation."

A denomination, however, must compete or die. No one is automatically a member of the Methodist Church, and the members of that Church must evangelize vigorously. In America mission and evangelism became synonyms! Competition between the denominations was the normal atmosphere which all churches breathed.

All traditions which came to America had to change. For those which were especially conscious of their ties with the past—Roman Catholics, Lutherans and Anglicans—change was often difficult and painful. But change they must. The pluralism of the new world, its vast space (unlike England where space was scarce) and its shortage of time (again unlike Europe where time was plentiful) meant that transition was inevitable.

The Episcopal Church shared in that transformation from establishment to denomination. Transition did not mean abandoning the past, at least for us. It meant adapting from the past. I am going to argue that we have gone through three major periods and are just entering a fourth. But in every one of those periods, including the present, I think that we have struggled with the question of relating our English past, our establishment past, to our American vocation.

The first period, the colonial period, was the longest—from 1607 until 1776 (or thereabouts), roughly 170 years. Eventually the thirteen English colonies saw the Church of England in America (as it came to be called) planted in all of them, though there was much variety from place to place. In some of the southern colonies the Church of England was established by law and (at least partially) in fact. Virginia and Maryland were the principal exhibits of an Anglican establishment. It is true that outside of Virginia, Maryland, and perhaps South Carolina, establishment was a facade with little life. But the ideal was very much alive.

That ideal was reflected in their understanding of mission. When they talk about mission, they sound very much like a church in England. In 1710 the vestry of Caratuck Parish in North Carolina wrote the Society for the Propagation of the Gospel (S.P.G.) that the Rev. James Adams

has during his abode here. . .behaved himself in all respects
as a messenger of the mild Jesus, exemplary in his life and
blameless in his Conversation; and now being bound for
England we with sorrowful hearts and true love and affec-
tion take our leave of him. . .a pious and painful [i.e., in-
dustrious] pastor whose sweetness of temper, diligence in his
Calling and Soundness of Doctrine has so much Conduced
to promote the great end of his Mission.[1]

And they went on to give as an example his more frequent
celebrations of "the Sacrament of the Lord's Supper."

When we move north, we find a somewhat different situation. Except for New York, the Church was not established
in the middle and New England colonies. Most of the congregations in Connecticut, New York, Pennsylvania, etc.,
were started by the first great missionary society of this
Church, the S.P.G. Just as two centuries earlier, Spanish
Catholicism had sent out its missionaries from one established church to create new, established churches from Mex-
ico to Manilla, so the Venerable Society sent out three
hundred priests, most of whom had grown up in England
and were conscious of its royal and public character, to plant
the Church of England.

Even though the pluralism of the middle colonies and the
congregationalism of New England made an establishment
unlikely, the most articulate of those priests never seemed
to lose the hope that an established church—as they had
known it and grown up with it—was the real vocation of the
Church of England in the Colonies. They preached to blacks,
started schools, nourished their congregations, and often had
nothing but contempt for "dissenters." One preacher in the
1760s assured his congregation that they were a "well-
ordered Society, a body of believers of which Jesus Christ
is the Head" in contrast to the "Conventicles of Hereticks
and Schismaticks, who, whatever they pretend, are really
not part of the Catholick Church. . .They are like a
Gangrened Member of the Body which receives no Nourish-
ment from the head."[2] The preacher's name: Samuel
Seabury.

53

This varied pattern with a common goal was brought to a sudden end when, as one S.P.G. priest wrote, the "spirit of disaffection and rebellion" (plus the essential aid of French power) won independence for the English colonies. Almost overnight the establishments in Virginia, Maryland, and elsewhere disappeared while those S.P.G. priests who continued to pray for the royal family could expect riots in their churches and the dispersion of their congregations. And so we begin the second period of our history which lasted, I suggest, from 1776 to about 1870.

We started, as usual, with about a twenty-year period of transformation. The years from 1776 to 1789 were crucial ones in this Church's history. The change took place with amazing speed, and by 1789 a new Constitution was agreed on and signed. The success of this transition is one of many signs of the basic health and vitality of the late eighteenth century church, and the new, somewhat defiant body chose a provocative name, The Protestant Episcopal Church.

The most important question which the newly organized Church faced was the question of identity. What made it distinctive? Why should it exist as a separate body? What could it offer in the new competitive and revivalist scene where the Second Great Awakening was about to begin?

Questions of identity are easily answered for established churches. The Church of England is (or rather was) simply the Church of the people of England. It could change considerably; Henry VIII might defend the pope, or later he might repudiate the pope, but the Church of England remained simply the Church of the English people.

Matters were not so simple for denominations, and every one which competed successfully developed clear images of identity with clear symbols and rites to express that identity. Think of the importance of adult baptism for the Baptist tradition—a powerful, distinctive, deeply personal experience. You knew you were a Christian and a Baptist when you went under in the river.

Episcopalians were not about to go under in the river. William White, Bishop of Pennsylvania, rector of Christ Church, Philadelphia, and the dominant leader in this Church for a generation, defined Episcopal identity in traditional terms. Our "enumerated particularities" were, he wrote, our liturgy, our articles (meaning the Thirty-Nine Articles), and episcopacy. If this was our identity, mission could not be far behind.

And indeed the second General Convention in 1792 adopted a statement on mission which reflected White's ideals.

However prosperous. . .the beginning of our Church in this new world, she will have little reason to look for a continuance of the Divine Blessing, if, when she contemplates so many members of her communion "scattered abroad, as sheep having no shepherd," she does not use her diligence to bring them within Christ's Fold, and to secure to them a stated administration of the ordinances of His religion.[3]

In an interesting and probably unconscious kind of way, this understanding of mission still looks back to an establishment mentality. Mission was addressed primarily to "members of her communion scattered abroad" and the purpose of mission was incorporation with the Church, to "bring them within Christ's Fold" and to the "ordinances of His religion."

That understanding of identity and mission had deep echoes in English history, but it carried little weight in the new country during the time of the Second Great Awakening. Who cared about liturgy or episcopacy when hordes of sinners, members of no communion, were unsaved and the New Testament alone was a guide to salvation?

So, it was a second generation of Episcopal leaders, men like John Henry Hobart of New York or William Whittingham of Maryland, who expanded White's "particularities" into a fuller imagery, the image of the apostolic Church. Why, Hobart and Whittingham asked, are liturgy and episcopacy important? Because, they answered, these were marks of the early church. Who understood the New Testament better than the early church? And of all the American traditions, none is more faithful to that early church than the Episcopal one. If you are serious about being faithful to the New Testament, you will inevitably seek out the Episcopal Church.

The vision of an apostolic church was hardly new, of course. Bishop Hobart probably learned it from Thomas Bradbury Chandler, and Bishop Seabury had preached about a "Catholick and Apostolick Church." But in a new age, when royal supremacy had to be jettisoned, Hobart, Whittingham, George Washington Doane and others sang the praises of an apostolic church with vigor and force.

I think this understanding of identity helps explain the new view of mission which developed in the 1830s. A voluntary missionary society was started by the General Convention of 1820, but it seems to have had little success. So the 1835 Convention, the Missionary Convention, adopted a new understanding of mission. As one evangelical priest put it, "Instead of a voluntary society, the Church [itself] is the Missionary Society." One church journal, *The Missionary*, saw clearly the connection between our identity as an apostolic church and our mission as a missionary church. The new vision of mission had power because it was apostolic.

The Protestant Episcopal Church in the United States has placed herself on primitive ground. She stands, as a Church, in the very attitude in which the Apostolic Church in Jerusalem. . .set out to bear the Gospel of its heavenly Head to every soul of man in every land. As the Church she undertakes, and before God binds herself to sustain, the injunction of her Lord, to go 'make disciples of all nations. . . .' Upon every one who, in the water of Baptism, has owned the eternal triune name, she lays, on peril of his soul if he neglect it, the same sacred charge. Her Bishops are Apostles, all; her clergy, all Evangelists; her members, each in his own sphere, and to his utmost strength, are Missionaries, every man; and she—that noblest of all names—a Missionary Church.[4]

Our understanding and our image of mission was to be expanded dramatically in the late nineteenth century, but it is necessary first to look a little deeper at the character of an episcopal and apostolic church if we want to see just how dramatic the changes were.

Episcopalians might argue that they simply reproduced the early and apostolic church, just as Baptists argued that they alone were the church of the New Testament; but neither could escape eighteen centuries of church history. The Protestant Episcopal Church that developed during that second great period was shaped as much by its own past as by loyalty to the apostolic church. Several characteristics stand out as dominant.

In the first place, it was argued, an apostolic church must be an unchanging church, and apologists gloried in the stability, the conservatism, the rock-like character of this Church. Indeed, the dominant image which emerged was that of the rock. As late as 1870, after the First Vatican Council, Anglican apologists bragged that not only was Protestantism a shifting scene but even Rome lacked stability, while nothing significant about the Episcopal Church ever changed. And externally, that was true. All efforts to revise the first Prayer Book of 1789 were resolutely stifled, canons were revised as little as possible, and the Thirty-Nine Articles were held up as an unchanging testament to fundamental New Testament doctrine.

In the second place, an apostolic church must have a uniform pattern of worship. Although church parties might emerge quickly, they would not be distinguished by different vestments or different liturgical practices. Apostolic worship turned out to be Morning Prayer, Litany, Ante-Communion and sermon, with the Communion service following about once a month. The surplice and scarf soon became universal, and the Protestant Episcopal Church was noted for its uniformity of worship from Boston to Georgia.

In the third place, an apostolic church lived its life separate from and uninvolved in any social or political issue. Bishop Hobart once wrote that a good churchman would so avoid politics that he would refuse to vote. I suspect that the source of this refusal had more to do with the Revolutionary War than with the apostolic church. Anglicans had been involved in a great political issue up to their elbows; unfortunately, many of them supported the losing side. There is an old Scottish proverb, "The burned child fears the fire." Anglicans had been badly burned, and—along with virtually every other American religious tradition—saw no need to interfere in politics or in social issues. To save the lost, to build up the church, to offer the liturgy faithfully and decently was more than enough.

In other words, during this second period, the theme of establishment seems to have been minimized, though not lost. Establishment had led to disaster at the end of the colonial period, and we had found a new, apostolic theme that was more relevant. We were an apostolic and missionary church, as the nineteenth century understood that term.

In the 1870s, however, the unchanging apostolic image came under irresistible challenges. Works by the new Biblical critics began to circulate here after the Civil War. They varied in quality and conclusions, of course; but all assumed that a centuries-old tradition of regarding the words of Scripture as dictated by God himself was wrong. The wrench for all thinking Christians was considerable. Episcopalians, for reasons I won't go into now, found it fairly easy to assimilate this new understanding. But in so doing, the image of an unchanging church was beginning to fade. Geology and biology also challenged almost universally held conclusions about the earth, about species, and about Biblical evidence. Darwin's *Origin of Species* was published in 1859 and his *Descent of Man* followed in 1871. Again, Episcopalians did not find it difficult to theologize about evolution; Darwin himself was buried in that holiest of Anglican burying grounds, Westminster Abbey. But to accept evolution not only meant that Episcopalians were changing their theology, it also—and more deeply—implied that evolutionary change instead of stability was built into the nature of things, perhaps even into the nature of a church.

But of all the challenges, none was more fatal to the Church of the Rock than the development of ritualism. By the 1870s, a small but significant number of priests and congregations had broken with the idea of a uniform liturgy and were enriching it in various ways. How central has our Prayer Book, our liturgy been? Virtually all of our great conflicts have been centered in questions of worship. When St. Mary the Virgin, New York City, was having Solemn High Mass with incense and vestments while St. George's was having Morning Prayer, Litany, Ante-Communion and sermon at the same time, the myth of an unchanging, uniform church was fatally weakened.

So, around 1870 we begin a third period which I call the national period and which lasted until around 1970. The two decades from 1870 to 1890 are fascinating because one can watch the transformation of an old image into a new one. Not only had the old myth of an unchanging, rock-like church become untenable, but great spokespersons—men and women—were ready to articulate a new vision.

Easily the most articulate was William Reed Huntington, rector of Grace Church, New York, and often described by contemporaries as the "most distinguished presbyter of the day." Huntington saw the mission of this Church as far more closely and creatively related both to national life and to all the American churches. His was a breathtaking vision—at times chauvinistic and racist—but awesome in its scope and grandeur nonetheless. For the mission of this Church was nothing less than to be (as he put in his most developed statement) "The National Church," responsible for the religious life and the leadership of the nation; and the basis for the reunion of all non-Roman, American Christianity. Establishment themes had returned in full force. Notice how this new understanding dealt with old problems.

First, ritualism was no longer a problem. A national church must be comprehensive, not uniform; and ritualism simply added to the richness of a comprehensive church. Again, the Thirty-Nine Articles were far too detailed and dogmatic to serve as a basis for the reunion of the American churches; and a new, more flexible, simpler confession was essential. Huntington had one in mind; he called it the Quadrilateral; and its four-sided argument still remains normative for this Church. Third, the Prayer Book, too, must be much more comprehensive and flexible; and one of Huntington's main goals was the revised Prayer Book of 1892, the first revision in our history. Or again, a national church must contribute to coping with national issues, and this Church moved from being selfconsciously apolitical to being at the forefront of the social gospel movement, much to the amazement—and sometimes delight—of non-Episcopal friends. A national church must have a National Cathedral, and we provided one in the national capital. A national church must prepare the leaders of the nation, and our great boys' prep schools did just that. And so on!

The vision of the national church was far richer than the hints I have given. Inspired by this vision (which had its

Anglo-Catholic as well as its evangelical versions), this Church grew in confidence and numbers. Indeed, for a brief period its growth was staggering—almost 50 percent a year! And its ability to attract national leaders and to play a key, a unique role in the ecumenical movement was noted by friends and foes alike. Its mission to shape the spiritual life of the nation was a dramatic success. The rewards in terms of both influence and numbers were substantial.

And then in the 1970s, the vision began to come apart! Why each of our visions should last for about a century I do not know; perhaps that is the normal life span of an Episcopal vision! But one hundred years after Huntington published *The Church Idea* in 1870—which was his first major statement of the national church myth—we entered a period of transition, turmoil and agony which has not ended.

Why so? What happened to our national vision? In the background of that vision, almost in our ecclesiastical collective unconscious, were some common assumptions, so common they were seldom challenged; indeed, seldom discussed. Let me tick off a few of those assumptions in the form they took during that third period:

The norm for this Church's actual worship would be Morning Prayer and sermon with music dominated by Anglican Chant.

Although women were important and valued members of the Church, their role was strictly subordinate. They were the Woman's Auxiliary. In many dioceses men alone could be elected to parish vestries; and throughout the period men only were eligible for election to the General Convention. The idea of ordaining women was never even discussed. This was a man-dominated ecclesiastical government.

A national church must support national institutions like marriage and the family, so this Church became—along with the Roman Catholic Church—the most rigid in the nation in its hostility to divorce. Virtually every parish of any size had a few members who were technically excommunicated. Having divorced and remarried, they might attend church; but they never came forward to receive communion.

There were other assumptions as well, but these are three significant ones. They have only to be mentioned to see why they were explosive. The changing, exploding world of the '60s and '70s saw every one of these assumptions sharply challenged. The Liturgical Movement held up another norm than Morning Prayer with Anglican Chant. Women would not rest content as an auxiliary to the church. Our position on divorce wreaked havoc in human lives as the divorce rate soared.

Even some of the boasts of the national church spokesmen had become a little hollow. To talk about this Church being uniquely responsible for the religious life of the nation now seems a little absurd. If a President wants to consult with a religious leader, he is more inclined to call Billy Graham or Jerry Falwell rather than the Bishop of Washington. Furthermore, Huntington's own racism is far more offensive today: he argued that one reason the Episcopal Church was to be a national leader was that it was composed mostly of the great Anglo-Saxon race! Or again, to describe our ecumenical role as being a "bridge church" (the favorite image even twenty years ago) is a little absurd when, for example, Roman Catholics and Lutherans are able to talk together without any help from bridge Episcopalians.

So, it seems to me that we are in the middle of a third and painful transition to a fourth period. A declining membership is only one sign of a deeper uncertainty of mission and identity. What is the Episcopal Church? What will be its identity and its mission in the future?

At this point, of course, I must leave my safe world of historical research and venture out into the exciting, but insecure world of prophecy. I do not know what the future holds. But I can make a few guesses.

A new identity always builds upon the past, reshapes the inheritance of the past. We began during the colonial period with the centrality of establishment. We moved on during our second period to emphasize our apostolic ties, our roots with the whole past of Christian history, our vision as in some sense a Catholic Church. During the third period, we rediscovered new riches in a combination of those two themes—a recovery and a new understanding of establishment which saw our mission as in some sense apostolic as well as national. That combination is our immediate heritage.

I suspect that the future will see a new combination of that same heritage. It will be new. The old chauvinism, "to reshape the spiritual life of the nation," along with the old conviction that we would soon be the largest church in the country is, I think, gone. We have learned, painfully sometimes, some humility. But, I suspect that our sense of having some responsibility for all the people of this land is not about to desert us.

And I think that our vision as an apostolic church is stronger than ever. In the beginning of the nineteenth century, we thought the apostolic church was monochrome, unchanging, rigid. And we were monochrome, unchanging, rigid. And just as we now know that in fact the apostolic church was extraordinarily varied, incredibly flexible, and given to much change, so our view of ourselves as apostolic is already a much more comprehensive, varied, and flexible one.

Just what that combination will look like, I do not know. But it is tempting to see in the two primates who will span our period of transition something of that combination. Bishop John Allin (1974-1986) was, to oversimplify a great deal, one who called us back to our apostolic roots. A new and very flexible Prayer Book, a call to mission, to evangelism, to holiness, to a venture in mission, were some of the high points of his tenure. The period of Bishop Edmond Browning is, of course, in the future; but some of his early statements suggest that he will probably emphasize more the establishment side of our past, our mission to national life, our vocation to be—along with other traditions— something of the conscience of the nation.

Of one thing, I think we can be sure. Either our corporate Christian life as Episcopalians has enough integrity for a new understanding of our identity and a new understanding of mission to be born, or we will cease to be in any significant way. No sizable group can survive in pluralistic America without a fairly strong sense of its own identity and its mission. Twice before in our history we have had to answer the questions of identity and mission. We did so in a creative and relevant way. And that process was followed each time by remarkably creative and positive developments for over a generation.

I think there is a growing vitality and commitment in this Church. So I think we can take hope from our past that we—and even more, our children—are entering into a rich, new and creative period in the ongoing mission of this Church.

End Notes

[1]John Frederick Woolverton, *Colonial Anglicanism in North America*, (Detroit: Wayne State University Press, 1984), 23-24.

[2]Ibid, 33.

[3]E. Cowes Chorley, "The Missionary March of the American Episcopal Church, 1789-1835," *Historical Magazine of the Protestant Episcopal Church*, 15 (1946):175.

[4]*The Missionary*, 1, No. 42 (1835), 167-168.

The Bishop as Chief Missionary

Richard F. Grein

When the title for this address, "The Bishop as Chief Missionary," was first proposed, I accepted the suggestion without having the least idea what I would say. Then, as I put my mind to the task, I immediately encountered a dilemma: As a missionary, it is easier to compare the work of Jackson Kemper to that of the Apostle Paul than to compare him with present day American bishops. Bishop George Washington Doane in his sermon at the consecration of Kemper made this distinction: "And this is what is meant by a missionary Bishop—a Bishop sent forth by the Church, not sought for of the Church—going before, to organize the Church, not waiting until the Church has partially been organized." This is a useful differentiation. Certainly the idea of missionary is essential to the office of bishop, if only because it is central to our understanding of the meaning of "apostle"—as the one sent on mission. But to go out personally to organize the Church in a totally new area by preaching the Gospel and establishing new congregations, is an experience as uncommon among our bishops as it was routine for Kemper and Paul.

My task, then, is not so much to compare the missionary work of Kemper with that of our American bishops. It is rather to capture some of the spirit and energy of that missionary church of 150 years ago and suggest some ways in which bishops today can initiate and participate in the missionary task.

Before I begin I want to put some limits on the subject at hand. First, regarding the term "missionary," because of its derivative relationship to our understanding of the Church's mission, broadly speaking, the term could be applied to anyone who is sent by the Church on mission. For example, missionary can refer to someone sent to render a specialized ministry of service, such as a medical missionary. But in keeping with the spirit of the General Convention of 1835 I want to focus my remarks on the role of missionary in its relationship to the growing edge of the Church; that is, to the evangelization and gathering of people for the growth of the Church, and the establishment of new congregations.

Second, in way of limitations, I want to focus my remarks on the bishop as missionary within the confines of his own diocese. I make this limitation because all bishops are, by virtue of their office, involved in the missionary work of the Church. As a sign of unity a bishop unites his diocese to the whole Church and its mission. He participates directly in those decisions which lead to new missionary efforts and in finding support for ongoing work. Also many of our dioceses have companion relationships with overseas dioceses, or support mission work around the world by sending missionaries and financial offerings. The bishop is a key figure in all of this. And this is important work.

Yet all too often many think of this sort of missionary activity as something we do somewhere else—not at home. It should be mentioned, however, that population shifts, growing metropolitan areas and the great influx of Hispanic people have recently awakened a new concern for domestic mission. And it is about domestic mission that I am primarily concerned in this paper. For it is within the boundaries of his own diocese that a bishop can truly be called "the chief missionary."

Let us begin, then, by noting that the General Convention of 1835 which elected Jackson Kemper as its first missionary bishop also reorganized the Domestic and Foreign Missionary Society. It defined the Society as being co-extensive with the Episcopal Church. These two actions of the General Convention had the effect of clearly declaring that this Church was a missionary Church, and that every member in it was a missionary, or at least had some kind of responsibility for ongoing missionary work. This vision, while true to the call of the Gospel, has rarely been adequately realized. I am not sure we will ever get to the point where even a majority of Episcopalians will begin to think of themselves as having a serious role to play in the missionary task of the Church. But I do believe it is possible to begin to do some things which will bring us a few steps closer to the ideal. And the key person in each diocese to facilitate such a process is the bishop.

At this point I want to offer an apology for selecting Church growth as my mission theme as a way of setting a context. Certainly one major factor in this selection is the person and events we celebrate—the expansion of the Church was part of their purpose. However, another and more immediate reason for this choice is because of what I perceive to be a prevailing disinterest in growth as a major goal for missionary activity within our own Episcopal Church. In part this attitude comes in the form of a subtle, even unconscious, resistance to any kind of evangelism; a resistance possibly formed in part as a reaction to fundamentalism's preoccupation with numerical growth, and its methodology.

But the real source of opposition to Church growth comes from those who claim that an emphasis on growth deflects the energies of the Church from more urgent objectives of mission. One Presbyterian minister writing in support of such a position said:

> *But church growth is not the point. The point is whether the church is being true to the Gospel. And, in city after city and town after town, it is. Indeed, because it is being faithful it is often losing members.*
>
> *Loss of growth in statistics has often meant increase in growth in the Gospel. The "dead wood" is gone. The "faithful remnant" remains. The church is lean and stripped for action. . . .*[1]

He goes on to say that "most churches could be two-thirds smaller and lose nothing in power." He fears that efforts to foster church growth will endanger personal growth, forgiveness, sensitivity, and discipleship. My fear is that this position is held by some within the Episcopal Church.

Apart from the fact that this attitude goes contrary to the clear command of the Gospel to go make disciples of all nations baptizing, and teaching, and is implicitly elitist, the real issue here is whether certain specific mission goals of the Church are only attainable at the cost of ignoring others. But let us try to raise the issue more concretely. Let us consider a few goals for the life of a parish—for example, numerical growth, effective social witness, nurture through pastoral care, training for discipleship, servant ministries, and the establishment of a warm, loving, caring community. The question is: Are these goals inherently mutually exclusive? Does the doing of some of them conflict with the doing of others? I think not. In fact, I would argue that such goals for mission are essential one to the other.

A recent study by sociologists and experts on church growth shows that growing churches have stronger commitment, greater unity and support, and a greater sense of satisfaction and enthusiasm among their members than do static or declining churches. The authors concluded their findings by saying:

> *To summarize, growth has little impact, either positive or negative, on a congregation's achievement of other goals. If anything, growing churches appear to be achieving other goals a bit better than those that are stable or declining in membership.*[2]

These findings would suggest that while growing churches are not axiomatically involved in other aspects of the Church's mission, they do have a greater capacity for a variety of mission goals and increased energy for carrying them out. What they need is the leadership to direct them to mission. Further, I would suspect that in many congregations where growth is static or declining often much of the energy of the people is directed toward survival goals—is turned inward rather than outward toward mission. Based on an assumption about human nature, I would also hazard a guess: Because people generally want to be worthwhile members of a worthwhile group, survival goals have little or no appeal to prospective new members. It is the sense of mission which is attractive.

All of this is to say that the various goals for the mission of the Church only come into conflict when we argue for them in terms of a primacy. And as we shall see later in this paper we cannot consider any mission activity, let alone numerical growth, until provision is made for pastoral care and formation of God's people. If the Church is to succeed in its mission tasks, there must also be a balancing concern for a sustained and spiritually maintained community. When all of this is understood in terms of balance, or as necessary parts of a whole vision for the mission task, they appear not as competing goals but as healthy tensions. They produce vitality.

But let us look at the problem of specific goals for mission from a slightly different perspective. The theological basis for the Church's mission is set forth in the life of Christ. Christology determines ecclesiology. As Anglicans we follow this rule in our fondness for describing the Church as the extension of the Incarnation. Following this description we could say that the mission of the Church is to reproduce the life of its Lord. Such a comprehensive vision for the Church transcends any particular goal for mission.

Yet because the Church needs to organize itself as any other institution, that is, it must administer its resources and plan its strategy, it must also declare its mission in terms of particular goals or objectives. The danger here is that amidst the particularity of institutional statements the comprehensive theological vision which gives life to mission will be forgotten. All too often the grand design for the Church falls victim to the human tendency for reductionism: "The real mission of the Church is. . ."; or, "The primary purpose of the Church is. . ."; or, "The most important aspect of our ministry to society is. . ." So that rather than seeking to climb the high mountain of our vocation in Christ, we reduce it to a manageable molehill and claim to be faithful to our call.

Another important question concerns the attitude we bring to mission—the posture the Church takes with regard to society. As the People of God respond to the call to mission, what perception concerning the relationship between Church and culture do they carry with them? This is an important question because that perception, whatever it might be, will determine the attitude which shapes and characterizes the ministry given. And this is particularly important where Church growth is concerned. For the thing we find offensive in many evangelists and evangelism programs is what they implicitly say about the nature of Christianity by what is said and done. We need to be careful here to distinguish between the mission itself and the way it is carried out—between the vocation to evangelize and the attitude and behavior of the evangelists. We ought not set aside that aspect of the mission of the Church oriented to growth just because we do not like the way some churches do it, or we do not like their attitude in doing it. Let us find a better way.

H. Richard Niebuhr, in *Christ and Culture*, discusses five ways of understanding the relationship between the Church and culture: Christ against culture, Christ of culture, Christ above culture, Christ and culture, and Christ transforming culture. Each of these, if taken seriously, would determine a particular kind of posture brought to the missionary task. They would range from elitist separation to complete accommodation.

I think it can be argued that our Anglican tendency to describe the Church in terms of the Incarnation leads us to the fifth of Niebuhr's five ways: Christ transforming culture. Given that, the question that needs to be raised is, What does the Church's mission look like if its purpose is the transformation of society? More explicitly, how will such an understanding of the relationship between Church and society shape and determine the mission goal of Church growth? Or to raise that same question in a slightly different way: If the Church is in some sense a continuation of the gift of the Incarnation, how can this understanding of "Church as gift" characterize our mission to evangelize?

It is not my purpose in this paper to attempt to answer these questions. I simply raise them because I believe them to be necessary considerations any time we set out on a mission of Church growth. They keep such a mission in perspective. And they point us toward a different way of carrying out the task—one more in keeping with our understanding of the Church and its mission.

All that I have said up to now in this apology for Church growth as a mission goal points toward a clear need: that is, a well-articulated ecclesiology. We need a clear vision of what the Church is called to be: a theology of the Church that is comprehensive enough to keep the various aspects of the mission task in balance, and which gives specific institutional goals a good theological context and rationale; and an ecclesiology which helps both the *laos* and those in holy orders have sense of role in mission, some sense of place in the Church's call. It ought in some way deal with the relationship between Church and society. Finally, it should be grand enough to inspire vocation and clear enough to be useful. I believe the person responsible for such an ecclesiology, and for its constant articulation in a diocese, is the bishop. This might be considered his first task as chief missionary. And it is very much in keeping with that question posed in the ordination rite for bishops: "Will you boldly proclaim and interpret the Gospel of Christ, enlightening the minds and stirring up the conscience of your people?"[3]

This brings us to what I perceive to be the second major task of a bishop seeking to be the chief missionary of a diocese: the formation of the People of God. Before the Church can be sent it must be nurtured, built up. Before the Church evangelizes others, it must itself be evangelized. Formation prepares the Church for its mission, and it also prepares a community to receive and nurture those brought to faith. It makes no sense for a parish or diocese to launch a program for Church growth if the congregations involved are not prepared to nurture people in all aspects of their baptismal profession. But it is precisely here, I believe, that we have failed.

A few years ago two sociologists by the names of Charles Glock and Rodney Stark, doing research on religion, wrote a book called *American Piety: The Nature of Religious Commitment.* Where the Episcopal Church was concerned, the findings of this book were very revealing. In a chapter entitled "The Switchers: Changes of Denomination," they state that of the denominations other than Roman Catholic, the one most able to retain its own members was the Episcopal Church. Conversely, among those best able to gain at the expense of other denominations was again the Episcopal Church. These results were based on percentage growth or decline. The authors had this to say:

The Episcopalians excelled in both ways: they held their original flock better than did the other denominations and they proved a strong attraction to members from other bodies.[4]

This, of course, fits with the statistic that 58 percent of our adult membership comes from other churches.

This does raise some questions for us: Why are we not growing? and, Where did all those people go? The answers to these questions are both complex and simple. When Episcopalians leave the Episcopal Church most often they do not go to any other church—they simply drop out. A great many continue to call themselves Episcopalians, but they are not counted on parish rolls. I have heard that there are more people claiming to be Episcopalians but not participating in a parish—lapsed members—than we count in our official statistics.

I mention this not because I think that a strategy to try and get these people back into active membership in the Church is a high priority. That would be an exceedingly difficult task for many reasons. But I mention this "leak" in our system because it points in a paradoxical way to one of our primary problems in mission strategy—that of pastoral care, the formation of the People of God—the gathered Church.

Even a cursory examination of the material on religious commitment in the Glock and Stark book reveals this problem of formation. The indices for devotional life, religious knowledge, and communal participation show Episcopalians to be at or near the bottom of the scale. Based on this evidence one could argue effectively that the basic reason for lack of growth in membership in the Episcopal Church is not only due to a poor sense of evangelism or lack of mission strategy, but because of inadequate Christian formation taking place in our local gathered communities.

The fact is that in recent history, as a church we have received new members from other churches at a rate out of proportion to our size, but have failed in our ministry to them and to those raised as Episcopalians. We have failed in the area of pastoral care.

I used the term "pastoral care" here intentionally, although for most in our church today it carries connotations of crisis ministry or caring for troubled people. Before the turn of this century pastoral care included all those elements of ministry within the gathered community which helped one grow

71

in Christ. What we now have is a therapeutic model of pastoral ministry oriented to people with problems, rather than a growth model. I think Boone Porter's editorial in the May 6, 1984, issue of *The Living Church* was exactly right. He said, "The ordained ministry of the Episcopal Church today is primarily a ministry of maintenance, not of mission."[5] We have put more emphasis on clinical pastoral education and crisis counseling than we have on training pastors to help people grow in their Christian life. How will we equip the saints for mission if we continue to ignore their formation?

We are fortunate that our present *Book of Common Prayer* provides the appropriate liturgical basis for proper formation to occur, and to foster a new sense of mission in the People of God. The eucharistic rite has received the most attention, and caused the biggest fuss, but I believe it is the rite of initiation which will have the biggest impact on the life of the Church. The regular and public rehearsal of the baptismal covenant has already begun to create a different understanding about the nature of ministry. The baptismal covenant makes it very clear that those who are baptized have responsibility to offer their lives in service to the Gospel. And even now more and more people are gradually coming to grasp the idea that the normal ministry of the Church is the ministry of the baptized. Thus what the Church teaches about mission is realized in the sacraments of initiation. This in and of itself will have the effect of bringing us closer to the ideal expressed in the General Convention of 1835.

Significantly, *The Book of Common Prayer* also clarifies and stresses the bishop's role as chief priest and pastor of a diocese. The evidence for this is most clearly found in the rite of ordination of a bishop, and in the rubrics for holy baptism and the eucharist which give the bishop special prerogatives in the liturgical life of the diocese. The bishop, then, is the one around whom the diocese gathers to celebrate the sacraments of redemption. He is the sign of unity in Christ, and the one through whom each member of the diocese is in communion with the whole Church.

But as the bishop gathers the Church, he also sends the Church. Listen to the prayer over candidates at confirmation, reception and reaffirmation:

Almighty God, we thank you that by the death and resur-
rection of your Son Jesus Christ you have overcome sin and
brought us to yourself, and that by the sealing of your Holy
Spirit you have bound us to your service. Renew in these
your Servants the covenant you made with them at their
Baptism. Send them forth in the power of that Spirit to per-
form the service you set before them; through Jesus Christ
your Son our Lord, who lives and reigns with you and the
Holy Spirit, one God, now and for ever. Amen.

And the words at the laying on of hands at Confirmation:

Strengthen, O Lord, your servant N. with your Holy Spirit;
empower him for your service; and sustain him all the days
of his life. Amen.[6]

As the apostle of mission he is not only sent by the Church,
he also sends the Church.

This double role as the one who gathers and sends the
Church is clearly expressed in the examination of the
ordination rite:

As a chief priest and pastor, will you encourage and support
all baptized people in their gifts and ministries, nourish them
from the riches of God's grace, pray for them without ceas-
ing, and celebrate with them the sacraments of our
redemption?[7]

The bishop as chief priest and pastor, and chief missionary is called upon to maintain the balance, the rhythm of
the Church's life—its gathering for worship and nurture and
its sending for mission. I have stressed pastoral care and formation because it appears to me to be a weakness that needs
attention if we are to be a missionary church.

Here I need to say a little bit more about what I mean by
pastoral care. By pastoral care I mean all those activities by
which pastors, bishops and priests, following the great commission of Christ, feed the flock of Christ. Or one could say
simply that it is the nurturing process that enables one to
live into his or her baptism—where baptism itself, or more
specifically, the Great Vigil of Easter, provides the pattern.
For it is here that we find the great themes of life: history,
story, and meaning; conversion, renunciation, and profession; identity, incorporation, relationship, and community;

73

purpose and vocation; faith and commitment; creation, dying and rebirth. Within the rhythm of gathering and sending, these great themes interpret and shape one's life. Pastoral care is the art by which this rhythm, pattern, and process is carried out.

Kierkegaard once said, "Life can only be understood backwards, but it must be lived forwards." This is one way to look at the relationship between the Church gathered and the Church sent. In gathering, the Church looks back into its tradition to "re-member" itself in Christ. The story is told and proclaimed in word and sacrament. The Church returns to its tradition to understand itself—for its identity. In this it has life. But it also lives by going forward—it lives by mission. And for this it is called.

The bishop's role in all this is to see that it takes place, to oversee it. To see that not only is there a balance in mission strategy, but a balance in the rhythm of gathering and sending. Clearly he cannot do this alone. Where pastoral care is concerned he must work with the presbyters of the diocese. As the ordination rite says, he is called to sustain his fellow presbyters and take counsel with them. For me this suggests a collegial relationship for the purpose of pastoral care.

This relationship is imaged in the ordination rite of priests in the laying on of hands. In fact, each of the three ordination rites expresses different kinds of relationships by the way hands are laid on. Bishops together lay hands on in the ordination of a bishop, expressing not only a continuity with the past in the historic succession but also a relationship of collegiality with each other in the life and work of the Church. Bishops lay hands on deacons alone because of the way deacons are called to relate to the bishop—"a special ministry of servanthood directly under the bishop." As Hippolytus says:

When the deacon is ordained, this is the reason why the bishop alone shall lay his hands upon him: he is not ordained to the priesthood but to serve the bishop and to carry out the bishop's commands. He does not take part in the council of the clergy; he is to attend to his own duties and to make known to the bishop such things as are needful.[8]

74

But priests are ordained in a collegial way by bishop and fellow presbyters. This ceremonial action points us toward a particular kind of collegial and corporate relationship; one, which in the words of Hippolytus, is of "the council of the clergy."

The question I want to raise, because I believe it relates to the bishop's role in pastoral care, is How do we socialize that which is imaged in the ordination rite of priests? How do we translate this ceremony into a personal and social reality? What I have in mind in raising this question is a movement away from the model where a bishop deals individually with the priests of a diocese, toward a more corporate, collegial model—such as a college of pastors working together to give pastoral care to a diocese. In such a collegial relationship a bishop could sustain and take counsel with priests. It would be a first step toward breaking down parochialism, a primary block to mission strategy. And it would provide a forum for developing and enhancing the art of pastoral care.

Thus far I have suggested two tasks for the bishop as chief missionary: As theologian to develop a theological model which will give clarity and life to the mission task; and as chief priest and pastor to the People of God. We now come to the third and final task, planning for mission.

Let me preface this section with a basic tenet for mission in general: The Church will not engage in mission unless it plans for mission. This seems obvious, but I am constantly amazed how few church institutions engage in long range, strategic planning. For example, unless an institution engages in serious budgetary planning at least five years out it cannot engage in serious mission strategy. This is because mission strategy requires a careful stewardship of resources. Budgets are mission statements! But to go back one step, budget planning requires institutional goals, clear statements of mission intentions. And goals require evaluation. This cycle of goal setting, stewardship of resources, and evaluation is called the planning process.

However, it is not my purpose here to get into intricacies of long range, strategic planning versus short range, planning processes. I am simply concerned that our attempts to be a mission church are more often than not hampered by haphazard, poorly conceived, unorganized attempts to carry out the serious business of mission. Church planning reminds me of some lines from *Alice in Wonderland*:

Said Alice to the Cheshire cat: "Which way
    shall I go?"
Said the cat: "Where do you want to go?"
"I don't really know," answered Alice.
"Then," said the cat, "if you don't know where you want to go,
    it doesn't much matter which way you go, does it?"

Simply put, planning is the process through which we decide where we want to go by setting goals. Then by utilizing resources and capacities, taking account of contingencies, we find the best way to get there. Without this process institutional management will tend to become immeshed in crisis administration. And more significantly, the primary mission of the Church will become its own continuation, having a set of unstated but dominating survival goals.

As chief missionary in a diocese the bishop is responsible for seeing that planning for mission takes place. He does not have to do it himself, but simply see that it happens. And I believe this includes a mission strategy for growth. Following our previous planning tenet: the Church will not grow unless it plans to grow. The consecration of Bishop Kemper was, after all, part of a plan for mission growth.

At this point I would like to make theory a little more concrete by sharing what we are doing in one diocese. One way we plan for Church growth in the Diocese of Kansas is by what we call "evangelism by strategic planning." This simply means that in growing areas we have a long range strategy for starting new congregations. And we have learned a painful lesson from the past 30 years of starting new churches— location is essential. Congregations which are not located on main streets or where they have high visibility will usually struggle for survival. Getting the right location means planning well in advance, at least ten years into the future. It means studying demographics, working with city planners, and buying building sites before the price of land forces the purchase of less desirable locations.

We have also learned that this sort of planning cannot be done out of the diocesan office in isolation from existing parishes. In the Episcopal Church our system of governance protects the autonomy of the various components of the Church: parishes, dioceses, and clergy. On the negative side this can produce isolationism and parochialism unless special effort is given to promote cooperation. We have had success asking parishes to work together in planning for mission using the diocesan staff as a support to the process. Several of our convocations have produced, or are producing, long range mission plans looking ahead fifteen years. These plans include such things as cooperative ministry programs, evangelism strategy, training for ministry, and location of new congregations. One convocation that includes a rapidly growing suburban area has developed a plan which caused us to move two parishes into better locations and they have selected areas where we need to build four or five churches in the next ten to fifteen years. This convocation has also already raised $250,000 for new work. The key here was nurturing cooperation in planning. Without this cooperation the existing six parishes could have felt threatened by the idea of new congregations and taken an adversarial stance.

But to go back to a point made previously about balance in the vision for mission. We cannot separate mission for growth from mission as a servant church. The growing suburb is bordered by a large inner city area undergoing change. The parishes in this area are struggling financially and unable to provide adequate ministry. We were very careful in planning to link our mission to grow with our mission to serve in the inner city. Each new congregation is being challenged with a sense of mission not only to grow but to serve. The inner city churches and the suburban churches are working together in planning for both the new developments and the ministry to a changing city. Such a holistic understanding of mission can only be accomplished by careful planning.

I have found that my job is to encourage local, cooperative planning for mission and ministry. It is sometimes painful, often slow, but always fruitful because it overcomes tendencies to parochialism.

The council in our diocese is elected by the convocations; it is a representative system. In other words, we have structured the diocese to support local mission. At the diocesan level we coordinate the plans of the convocations and act as stewards of diocesan resources to help finance their work by careful planning of budgets, at least five years out. The council is presently putting together a process to produce a twenty-year plan. This plan will be produced in cooperation with the convocation planning groups so that it will support and enable their efforts. In this way diocesan goals are not imposed from on top but become part of a total program for mission.

Well, enough of what we are doing in Kansas. I think you get the picture of how planning for mission can begin to produce cooperation and vitality.

About the time I began writing this paper the historiographer of the Diocese of Missouri, Charles Rehkopf, sent me a book entitled, *Recollections of a Missionary in the Great West*—published in 1900. He sent it to me because it was dedicated to the second Bishop of Kansas, Elisha Smith Thomas. I want to quote just a few lines from the book. They lend a degree of perspective to the theme of this conference and this paper.

Western dioceses are bishop-killers at best. No, that is unjust. It is the Church herself which kills her bishops. She puts them in positions where their faculties are taxed to the utmost naturally; she gives them rank, position, a bare living; and then she loads upon their shoulders, if they be men, as they always are, who see the opportunities, accept the responsibilities, and endeavor to fulfill the obligations of their position, burdens too heavy for any mortal man to bear. She provides them with little money, a mere pittance in comparison with their needs, gives them a few men, not always those best suited to effectually advance the work, and expects them to go forward.

If those Western bishops are not walking in apostolic footsteps, I know of no men who do so walk. It is the most exhausting, wearying, heartbreaking lot that can fall to any

> mortal man, to be a Western missionary bishop, and most
> of them fight it out until they die. The people are helpful,
> grateful, and appreciative. They do what they can. Let none
> blame them.

> The footprints of civilization are those made by the feet of
> the men who stand beautiful upon the wild prairies and high
> mountain-tops of the West, and bring good tidings, that pub-
> lish peace, that cry unto Zion, "Thy God reigneth.". . .9

This description of the western missionary bishop's labors,
though done in the heroic and dramatic style of the time,
does hold up before us an accurate picture. In this it keeps
us from overly romanticizing the past. And more import-
antly, it makes the necessary point that when the Church
engages in mission it engages in hard work. There are no
shortcuts, no grand designs by which the task is made easy.
After all the plans and preparations are made, it is people
who do mission. Individuals, called of God one by one, give
life to the Church's work.

What I have outlined in this paper is not a guide to
success—that we must leave to God in his own time. What
I offer are some suggestions for the bishop of a diocese who
wants to function as the chief missionary. In a brief apology
I tried to stress the importance of Church growth as an important mission task for the Episcopal Church. I would not
give it primacy. But because it has been largely neglected for
too long a time, we need it for balance. The rest of what I
have said could apply equally as well to any aspect of mission. I have also tried to emphasize the importance of the
articulation of a clear, useful ecclesiology to hold the vision
of mission in focus. Fundamental to the Church sent is the
Church gathered. Mission requires the building up of the
Church through pastoral care. Finally, I have stressed the
significance of planning. These suggestions all have the
underlying purpose of making it possible for the People of
God to engage in mission. At most, we can say they are ways
by which a bishop can seek to lead the Church on mission.
But finally the hard work of the mission itself must be left
to *laos*—the holy People of God.

End Notes

[1]Robert K. Hudnut, *Church Growth Is Not the Point* (New York: Harper and Row, 1975), ix.

[2]Wade Clark Roof, et al., "Factors Producing Growth or Decline in United Presbyterian Congregations," *Understanding Church Growth and Decline, 1950-1978,* ed. Dean R. Hoge and David A. Roozen (New York: The Pilgrim Press, 1979), 207.

[3]*The Book of Common Prayer* (New York: Church Hymnal Corp., 1979), 518.

[4]Rodney Stark and Charles Y. Glock, *American Piety: The Nature of Religious Commitment* (Berkeley: University of California Press, 1968), 187.

[5]*The Living Church,* 6 May 1984, 11.

[6]*The Book of Common Prayer,* 418.

[7]Ibid., 518.

[8]*The Apostolic Tradition of Hippolytus,* trans. Burton Scott Easton (Cambridge: The University Press, 1934), 38.

[9]Cyrus Townsend Brady, *Recollections of a Missionary in the Great West* (New York: Charles Scribner's Sons, 1900), 197-198.

The Frontiers of
Mission and Theology

James E. Griffiss

I want to begin this lecture by quoting the first stanza of
a once popular hymn, which has, I am sure, inspired many
with the challenge and romance of foreign missions.

From Greenland's icy mountains, from India's coral strand,
Where Afric's sunny fountains, roll down their golden sand.
From many an ancient river, from many a palmy plain,
They call us to deliver their land from error's chain.
Can we whose souls are lighted with wisdom from on high,
Can we to men benighted, the lamp of life deny?

The hymn was written by Reginald Heber in 1819 at the be-
ginning of the great surge of missionary activity by the
Church of England which was to dominate the 19th century.
It was written also at the time when the British Empire was
developing in Africa and the Far East. It reflected the attitude of many in the Church of England and, later, in the
Episcopal Church in this country towards missionary activity.
That attitude identified the Christian Gospel of salvation
with western civilization and especially with the virtues of
Anglo-Saxon culture. It was also tied up with political and
economic values; missionaries were both chaplains to the
British military and government officials as well as preachers
of the Gospel to the natives. Under such circumstances it
was easy to identify the Gospel with the values represented
by the empire. Such an attitude towards missionary activity
took a long time in dying, and it may to some degree still
be with us. There are those who would argue, for example,
that the Protestant missions to Latin America well into this
century, and perhaps even now, were not unrelated to the
economic exploitation of Latin peoples by American economic and political interests. I suspect such is the case from
personal experience because I spent some ten years teach-

ing in the Caribbean, and I discovered during the time that it was not always easy to distinguish between the Gospel as it was being preached in many churches (both Protestant and Catholic) and the anti-communism which has dominated American policy in the Caribbean and Central America.

But most significantly of all, perhaps, the hymn represents a fundamental attitude to a way of understanding the Gospel of salvation itself. It is saying that we Christians have the complete truth of divine revelation, and that it is our duty and responsibility, therefore, to give it to those who do not have it. All who are outside the Christian dispensation, in other words, are benighted; they live in darkness and error. The purpose of missionary activity, as the 19th century Church understood it, was to make truth and salvation available to others—a salvation which was more often than not identified with the future hope of heaven rather than with changing life in this world. Such an attitude towards missionary activity meant that there was a clear sense of purpose; missionaries knew what their mission was: to convert the heathen in order that they might be saved from error's chain and to bring them a truth which they could not otherwise have. And even as late as this century there remained the hope that the world could be converted to Christ in our own time and on those terms.

It is easy for us at the end of the 20th century and after so many changes in our world, to ridicule both the hope and the theology which Heber's hymn reflected. It is certainly not my intention to do so, however. We should not ridicule the 19th and early 20th centuries' notion of mission for the simple reason that with all of its faults it accomplished much and, indeed, its very success has created many of the challenges and opportunities which we have at the present time. Because of such missionary activity there is no continent left where the Gospel has not been preached and the Church planted. There are still many who are not Christian, but some of the earlier goals have been accomplished. And certainly some of the most vital and committed Christian communities—those in Africa, for example—owe their origin to the missionaries of the 19th century, whatever other problems they may have inherited from the political and economic policies which the missionaries brought with them. Clearly, also, human beings in many parts of the world have benefited from the educational and medical work of missionaries, and to some degree, although it is often hard to discern, the demand for economic and social justice in Africa, India, and South America can be traced to the preaching and teaching of those early missionaries.

As I have said, it is precisely the success (without considering the problems) of 19th and early 20th century missions which has created the challenge for us today in understanding what we mean by Christian missionary activity and how to go about it. I well remember, when I was sent off as a missionary appointee to Puerto Rico in 1961, being told by my bishop that I was to go to Puerto Rico to teach the natives the Christian religion while sitting, if necessary, under a palm tree. I knew enough to know that was not what it was all about—for one thing Puerto Ricans had been Christians for several centuries—but I knew very little about being a missionary or how to go about it. The challenge for us, of course, and the problem as well, is that we are no longer taking the Gospel to foreign parts; no parts of the world are foreign to the Church any longer. Nor are we out to convert the heathen from their benighted ways; the benefits of western civilization are not as unambiguous as they were thought to be in the 19th century. Therefore the heritage for us of 19th century missionary movements is that conversion, salvation, and mission itself must now be seen in different and, I think, more difficult terms.

In what follows I want to focus on what is called domestic mission; that is, the mission which the Episcopal Church has to the vast number of people here at home who, while they may admit to a belief in God and may even identify themselves with a particular religious tradition, nonetheless have very little awareness of the Gospel of salvation and of its consequences for their lives. I do so for two reasons: first, because foreign missions present a particular set of problems, it would not be possible to deal with both domestic and foreign missions in one short lecture; and second, because foreign missions are still perceived by many as exotic and romantic, whereas the mission to city or suburb can be thought rather humdrum, I think the perceived humdrumness of domestic mission may help us to see more clearly what the frontiers of mission and theology really are for us at the end of the 20th century.

The way in which many in the Church now understand mission is in terms of church growth through evangelism, and there are various techniques and programs for fostering church growth. I would not want to disparage any of those, because obviously we do want the Church to grow: we need to establish new congregations and to find ways of reaching the unchurched. There is, of course, an ever-present danger in the notion of church growth through evangelism if it should become growth for growth's sake, without any clear pastoral or theological foundation, and if it should become too concerned with statistics and ego-building for the clergy and lay leaders. But at its best mission through evangelism is seriously concerned with preaching the Gospel of salvation to those who need to hear it. However, whether fortunately or unfortunately, I do not think that evangelism, as it is practiced by many Christian groups (I am thinking here of television evangelists and the many pentecostal churches which are flourishing in suburban America), will ever be the chief focus for the missionary activity of the Episcopal Church in the United States, and, indeed, I believe it would be a mistake both theologically and pastorally for us to enter into competition with those groups. For one thing, many Episcopalians have fled from those churches which are very evangelical because they desired a more intellectual and less emotional form of religious practice. For another, our more ordered and stable form of church polity does not lend itself to spontaneous growth. Our initial evangelization of the Northwest Territory by Jackson Kemper, for example, with all of its success, reflected such an attitude. Kemper was consecrated a bishop, and he founded churches; he was not an evangelist in the style of many of those who preached on the frontier during the early period of expansion in the West. Indeed, it was precisely this issue—free preaching or the established order of parish churches—which had led to the schism between Methodists and Anglicans in the 18th century. The Methodists in England and later in this country had insisted upon their right to preach the Gospel outside of the confines of the parish church, and when the Methodist movement reached the United States that insistence continued in the evangelical work of itinerant preachers. But the Episcopal Church, reflecting its heritage in the Church of England, has never been comfortable with evangelism which did not lead to the participation of the converted in the regular and ordered life of the local congregation.

Such an attitude could be the result of our Anglican smugness and self-satisfaction, but I believe there is a deeper and more serious theological reason. The reason arises from what we believe about the Church, both in the narrow sense of the Episcopal Church and in the broader sense of the Catholic Church, because our sense of mission ought to be related to our theology of the Church.

We Anglicans have inherited a long tradition in our understanding of the Church. At times we have lost sight of it, and oftentimes we have not quite known what to do with it, but it is a tradition which has profoundly affected our way of being in the world. It is a tradition which goes back to the earliest days of Christian history when Christian people were struggling to understand what they believed about salvation in Jesus Christ, the presence of the Spirit in their lives, and the relationship of both to the community of people who gathered together for word and sacrament. What they came to see and what they continued to develop in theology, worship, prayer, and action was that the Church is the sacramental presence of Christ in the world through the indwelling presence of his Spirit and the means through which all men and women could be incorporated into Christ and enter into union with God. The foundation for their theology of the Church was their belief about the nature of Christ as the Incarnation of the Logos and Son of God, the second person of the Trinity. In the Incarnation, as Christian theology finally expressed it doctrinally, the eternal Logos and Son, who is one with God the Father, had taken on our humanity in the historic life of Jesus, so that all human beings have proleptically, that is, by promise and anticipation, received the benefit of Christ's redeeming work: in the Incarnation humanity has been redeemed, not just certain individuals. In a theme constantly repeated by the Fathers, St. Cyprian could say that the Church is the sacrament of our unity with Christ because it is now the cause, expression, and symbol of the final unity of all people with God among themselves through their sharing in the unity of the holy Trinity.[1] The Church for the Fathers was not simply an organization of men and women with a common purpose, nor just a place where moral principles could be taught and upheld. Rather it was to be thought of as a sign to the world of Christ's universal gift of salvation and the means through which all human beings could be united to God. Through Baptism and Eucharist, the two great sacramental acts, Christian people became a sign to the world of their common calling to share in the divine life. As one of the Fathers said of Christ: "The Son of God became son of man [that is he took our common humanity] so that the sons of men, that is, of Adam, might become sons of God...partakers of the life of God....Thus He is Son of God by nature, and we by grace."[2] The Church is the community empowered by the Spirit through which God's plan of redemption is carried out to "all sorts and conditions of men" and to all structures of society.

This "high" doctrine of the Church as the presence of Christ in the world and as a sign of the unity of all people in God continued in our own Anglican Fathers, especially Richard Hooker and Lancelot Andrewes in the 16th and 17th centuries. As one writer on Bishop Andrewes has said: "By...rooting the Christian life in the Church's corporate experience of the Holy Spirit, Andrewes presents the Church as a pre-eminently charismatic place. To be a member of the Body of Christ is to be the temple of the Holy Spirit. The Church is the place where the Spirit is present as God's gift, and as such the sphere in which Christ is to be encountered."[3] In a similar way Hooker wrote of the unity of the Father, Son, and Spirit as the basis for the Church and for our participation in Christ brought about by the gift of the Spirit. In the *Laws of Ecclesiastical Polity* he wrote: "[We can see] what communion Christ has with his Church, and his

Church and every member thereof is in him by original deri-
vation, and he personally in them by way of mystical associa-
tion wrought through the Gift of the Holy Ghost. . .till the
day of the final exaltation to a state of fellowship in glory,
with Him whose partakers they are now in those things that
tend to glory."[4] The Church shares in the reality of the Incarnate Christ as he shares in the reality of God. In Christ
all human beings are now called to share in the divine life;
to bring their calling into its fullness is the purpose of the
Church in the world and the reason for its existence.

Such a tradition of the Church has dominated much in
Anglican thinking, and it has had its consequences for the
way in which we think of the mission of the Church. There
are many examples from which one could choose, but the
most obvious is Frederick Dennison Maurice in the 19th century. In his *Kingdom of Christ*, first published in 1838 (just
a few years after Jackson Kemper's consecration as the first
missionary bishop of the Episcopal Church), Maurice ex-
plored "the idea of a Church Universal, not built upon
human inventions or human faith, but upon the very nature of God himself, and upon the union which he has
formed with his creatures; a Church revealed to man as a
fixed and eternal reality by means which infinite wisdom had
itself devised."[5] Maurice's theology of the Church in combination with the best insights of the Catholic Revival led to
a development in Anglican thinking which is still very much
with us. It was and continues to be a sense that the Church
is a present sign to the world of the salvation and hope which
God in Christ wills for all human beings and which he is
accomplishing through the power of the Spirit. It has led
to that peculiar "Anglican worldliness" which refuses to
make sharp distinctions between the saved and the damned,
between pagan and Christian, converted and unconverted,
but rather which sees the redeeming work of Christ present
to all human beings. For Maurice and many others the sacrament of Baptism is the mark of the Church, as a sign set
in the midst of the world, of the continuing presence of
Christ by his Spirit, the extension of the Incarnation, and
the sacrament of God's universal care and redemption. To
enter the Church through Baptism is not to leave the world

behind but to become a sacrament to the world. As Maurice said: "The world contains the elements of which the Church is composed. In the Church, these elements are penetrated by a uniting, reconciling power. The Church is, therefore, human society in its normal state; the World, that same society irregular and abnormal. The world is the Church without God; the Church is the world restored to its relation with God, taken back by him into the state for which He created it."[6]

For those who stand in it—and it represents, I would suggest, the best in the Catholic Movement in the Episcopal Church—this tradition has given us a sense of responsibility to the world which is not a denial of the political and social realities of the world, but rather one which seeks their transformation through witness and service in the political and social spheres. A sense of the transformation of political and social structures, rather than the conversion of individuals from an unredeemed state to a redeemed one, can very much affect how we ought to think of the mission of the Church. It does not mean that we should see ourselves in opposition to those in a more evangelical tradition, but rather parallel to them, carrying out a kind of mission on the frontiers of American life for which we as Anglicans may be especially well suited. It is, I would say, a more theological mission because it calls for a theological analysis of society and its problems.

The frontier to which Jackson Kemper carried the Gospel and on which he established new congregations no longer exists, but there are many other frontiers to which we, his spiritual descendants, have a mission today. To neglect those frontiers would not only be a denial of Bishop Kemper, but even more it would be apostasy to the Incarnate Lord who has redeemed all human beings. The new frontiers are perhaps more hidden, but they are nonetheless real. They are frontiers which, if we seek them out, will call us as a Church to witness to the care of God for all his people through our mission of service and our faithful offering of prayer. And, if we seek them out, they are frontiers which will call us also to live out in our life as a Church the radical meaning of the cross and resurrection, the only ground of

Christian hope. It is, I believe, the missionary responsibility of the Episcopal Church to seek out those frontiers and to bring to them the healing and saving power of the Incarnate Christ. I want to suggest several examples of those hidden frontiers which I believe can call us out of our complacency and smugness as a prosperous and quasi-established Church and which can give us a new sense of our mission.

There is, first of all, what is known in New York City as the "Minnesota Strip," although its equivalent can be found in every major city and in many small ones as well. It is the place to which boys and girls have fled from the banality or horror of their lives, and where they sell themselves out of despair and hunger or out of anger and indifference. Of course, such places have always existed in every city in the world, but we in the United States claim to be a nation which extols traditional family values and which, when it is useful for political purposes, can speak loftily of religious virtues and morality as the foundation of our society. Such unexamined rhetoric can only lead to further cynicism and despair, not only for the boys and girls themselves and their patrons, but also for those who attempt to minister to them. We must ask ourselves, What is the relationship between the Church, as the sacramental sign of God's care, and a society—of which we are all a part—which is dishonest and uncaring about the reality of human exploitation? This is a theological frontier of the most demanding kind.

There are many places, not only in foreign parts but here at home as well, where human greed and hypocrisy mean that people are starving to death and where the elderly and sick in an affluent and militaristic society such as ours are tormented by loneliness, despair, and fear, who suffer cold and hunger while so many of us live in comfort and security. What is our mission as Christian people and as a Church in a society which would appear to have forgotten the Gospel command to care for those in need?

What is our mission as a Church on the frontiers of medical research, nuclear warfare, and all those other complex areas in which human life is threatened or its value disregarded? Can we justify exorbitantly expensive medical care for a few, while denying it to many who are poor? Can we, on the one hand, oppose abortion while, on the other hand, advocate capital punishment or a "first strike" nuclear policy? What, in other words, does the Gospel say to us about the value of human life and our actions for it or against it?

And lest we forget it, there are many affluent suburbs and small towns with pleasant and successful churches where people are being destroyed by drugs or by the hatred and scorn of their neighbors or by the sins of complacency and indifference. Too often when people turn to the Church for help or for judgment they find a people turned in on themselves and unwilling to face the reality of human pain and sin. How can a local congregation minister to those next door, our neighbors, who stand in need? Here again is a frontier to which we are called, because we are a parochial and parish church.

Obviously, these are only a few of the frontiers to which the Church has a mission—there are many others. And, as I have said, they are frontiers which are not exotic and romantic, nor can they provide us with much satisfaction for a job well done. The sad thing is that they are frontiers which seem to have no solution. There is no plan or program which can answer the questions I have raised. They will always be the questions which will challenge us no matter what government is in power. What then is our mission to such frontiers and how do we engage them theologically and without despair?

As we seek to answer that question our understanding of the nature of the Church can guide us. If we believe that the Church is the sacramental sign in the world of God's redeeming work for all humanity in the Incarnation, then we shall see our mission as one of being a sign to the world of what God in Christ has done and will do for us and for all those in hopeless despair. It can help us to see that the primary goal of our mission is not church growth for its own sake, but to be a witness of hope through our service to others and through our prayer for them and with them.

Serving others in the name of Christ can take many forms: strategies for evangelism, building hospitals and schools, operating a soup kitchen, caring for the sick, and being present with those in need. But all of those activities derive from our theological understanding of the Church. If we understand the Church as a sign to all human beings of God's providential care for them, then we are primarily called to a mission of *diakonia*—service to those in need, whatever the need may be. Because we have known God's care incarnate in Jesus Christ, our mission in word and action ought to be to make his care visible in the lives of others. I want to suggest three characteristics of such caring for the world in the name of Christ—characteristics which will work themselves out in various concrete ways.

First, our mission of service must be characterized by our willingness and our ability to give expression to God's judgment upon human sin and his forgiveness freely given in Jesus Christ. As Christians we know in our own lives in the Church something of judgment and forgiveness; we acknowledge our sins and we know the free gift of forgiveness. But because we know both in our own lives we ought also to know how difficult it is to give expression to them in the complex issues facing our society. It is especially difficult to do so for those who live on the hidden frontiers of American life, for in those places of poverty, despair, violence, selfishness and fear, how people act can more easily call forth a word of judgment, and the word of forgiveness can be much harder to speak. How can we speak the word of forgiveness to those who destroy others, who use other people wantonly or as a matter of personal convenience? On the other hand, how can we speak the word of judgment to those in power who would deceive us with promises of security through greater nuclear power or economic strength? Both words need to be spoken for they are the words of the Gospel: God's judgment upon human sin and his free offer of forgiveness. The mission of the Christian community in its witness of service is to find the way to speak both words to those on the hidden frontiers as well as the more obvious frontiers of power in American society.

Second, our mission of service must be characterized by poverty. This may sound an odd thing to say to a group of Episcopalians, all of whom are financially comfortable in comparison to a great many people in this country. But poverty, as we are so often taught in Scripture, means much more than our financial situation. It means being able to show in one's life that there is no security, no strength, except in that which is given to us in Christ. Poverty of spirit means to know that our only foundation is the cross. In this area we Episcopalians in the United States must face many of the issues which are being addressed by our fellow Christians in Europe, Africa, and Latin America, namely, to engage the serious social and political issues of our society from the foundation of our faith in the crucified Christ—the one who was without power, who gave his life for others, and who identified himself with the outcasts. The radical question of the Gospel is, On what do we depend as a Church and as individuals, and, therefore, on what ought our society itself depend? This mission of service to ourselves and to society is not one of offering facile answers to hard economic and political questions. Most theologians and preachers, as well as most laypeople, are not economists or politicians. But all of us do have the mission to ask theological questions of economists and politicians, as difficult as that may be, for we have the mission to serve ourselves and our society by learning to live the meaning of spiritual poverty in an affluent and materialistic nation, one which seeks security in more nuclear arms, social welfare programs, a balanced budget, or the rule of law and order and larger prisons.

Finally, our mission of service to others means that we must be a community in which the presence of the Spirit is evident to all who see us. The term "presence of the Spirit" can, of course, have a bad connotation. It can suggest the more extreme aspects of the charismatic movement, or an un-worldly or other-worldly attitude towards the pain and suffering of human beings, one which ignores the present world and fixes its attention only on another world—what has aptly been described as a "pie in the sky" spirituality. Neither of these, and most certainly not the second, is the way to show the presence of the Spirit of God in the Church. The Spirit is the continuing and power-filled presence of the risen and ascended Christ, who now fills the whole earth. The Spirit is the witness to God's transcendent reality and to his presence with all human beings and all human communities. Many human beings do not know the Spirit of God, and it is the mission of the Church to make his presence known and believed. Our mission must be seen not simply as taking God to those who do not know him, but rather of enabling them to discern the Spirit in the signs of their own times.

I think the chief area in which our witness to the Spirit is our primary mission is to find the way to show others that there is more to the world and more to human life than our society is often willing to admit. It is to say that there is value and care at the heart of reality and that morality, duty, love, and freedom are not simply capricious or trivial; rather it is to say that they are at the heart of reality because they are at the heart of the God who is present with us in the Spirit. In the Church we know that there is more to reality than just the outward appearances would suggest. We know such things because we believe that water and bread and wine open us to a reality which transcends the space and time of our lives. And we believe also that human beings, in all their complexity and sin, are called to share in the divine life through the power of the Spirit. For that reason our mission is to witness to the value and integrity of every human life no matter how distorted it may be by sin or no matter how much it may be scorned and rejected by the self-righteousness of others. Here again our mission is theological, for it means discerning the presence of God in all those who have been rejected or forgotten in our society, as well as all those who with power and money hunger for God. How to engage our mission to all of them requires of us that we discern the presence of the Spirit in our lives and in the Church. Such discernment is theological, because it involves what we believe about God.

The second dimension of our mission is prayer, for prayer is the action of the Church which draws together all the characteristics of our service to others. Because we see the Church in terms of the Incarnation and the sacramental life our prayer in the Church has a certain structure or character to it which is vital for our understanding of our mission of prayer. The Incarnation says to us that the God who gives himself to us in Jesus Christ is the one who, in many different ways, gives himself to all human beings so that all men and women have some experience of him and some relationship with the transcendent mystery of God, a mystery fully made known to us in Christ but present, however unknown, in the lives of all people. To say otherwise would be to deny that God is the creator of heaven and earth and the end and perfection of all things. In Jesus Christ, we believe, our human nature and human history, the humanity of every person there is, is taken up into God and united with the Father through the Son. "God was in Christ," Paul says, "reconciling the world—that is, all human beings—to himself." In the Spirit we are made able to believe such things, to call Jesus Lord, and so in the Spirit we are made able to pray to the Father in, through, and with Jesus who is one with the Father and one with us. It is to such a belief that the Church witnesses in its mission of prayer.

As Christians we are not praying across a gulf, to a God far off. We are praying with the God who has taken our common humanity, who prays with us in the Spirit, and who offers himself with us as we pray and offer with him. Such a belief has consequences for the form and structure of our prayer as we pray not only for ourselves but much more for those men and women who do not yet believe, who do not know how to pray, and who live on the frontiers of our society. It affects the way we pray to realize that we pray as the human beings we are; all that goes to make us who we are is, through the Incarnation, present to the Father in Jesus Christ through the praying of the Spirit in us. But even more, prayer through Jesus Christ is not just the individual isolated petition of those who believe. Prayer is the offering of the risen Christ to the Father for the whole creation, so that our prayer in the Church, which is his Body, is the offering of our common humanity—a humanity called into being in his cross and resurrection. Our prayer carries with it and offers with it the prayer, articulate or inarticulate, a word spoken or only a cry of despair, of every human being because we all share in the humanity of Christ. The pain and suffering, as well as the joy, of every person are present to the Father through the prayer of the Church, just as our pain, suffering and joy are present to the Father through the prayer of others. Because we who believe pray in, through, and with Christ and the Spirit we are praying with all men and women who do not yet believe, and we share with them who they are and who they are called to become in Christ.

Our service to others through our willingness to speak God's word of judgment and forgiveness, through our poverty, and through our spirituality is drawn together in prayer as the offering of our common humanity to God the Father through Jesus Christ. That service shapes our prayer as we bring the questions, doubts, sufferings of all human beings and offer them in Christ to the Father. Human beings do not all have the same needs nor the same images and concepts of themselves and of God. We may not like what shapes our prayer from the frontiers of American society—the drug addict, the prostitute, the sick and suffering, the victim of AIDS who is homeless and despairing, as well as the mindless joy or upward mobility of many in suburban and urban America; but for those of us who believe our mission to be one of witness through service and prayer, those needs and many others must shape our prayer because they shape the lives of those with whom we pray through Jesus Christ and in the Spirit. It is easy to pray for those we love or admire, and of course we must; but the mission of the Church, and especially as I have suggested of the Episcopal Church, is to learn to pray for all of those on the frontiers of American life. That may well be our particular mission because our doctrine of the Church has been so grounded in the Incarnation as a way of seeing and understanding the unity of all people in Christ and their common call into the divine life. Such prayer is mission because it is the act of Christian hope in a frequently despairing world.

Christian belief is that hope conquers despair, that life conquers death, that God's rule and kingdom will come, and that there will be life-giving bread and life-giving blessings. To despair in the face of the frontiers of America—and of the world—is much easier, because the other name for despair is indifference. Hope for us in the last part of the 20th century, as we respond to our mission, is much more difficult than it was during the period of missionary expansion in the last century. Then it seemed that if we all worked hard, gave our money, and sent out missionaries to foreign parts sin and evil could be eradicated, nonbelievers converted, and we could all enjoy the blessings of peace and prosperity. But such optimism and illusion have died for us after two world wars, the holocaust, the threat of nuclear destruction, and all the other ills which afflict us. But indeed that illusion ought to have died long ago for Christian people on the cross, for the reality of the cross destroys all of our romantic illusions about mission and Church growth. Jesus died on the cross and his death must always be the only center of our hope, for only in the cross can the reality of human horror, suffering, pain, and indifference be confronted with the life of the resurrection. And that is what the Church is called to proclaim in its mission: we are a small group of people witnessing, serving, and praying in the face of the desperate need of millions on the frontiers, and we are called to do so, without hypocrisy and without illusion, in order that we shall be able to say, We believe in the resurrection of the dead and the life of the world to come.

End Notes

[1]Cyprian, *De catholicae ecclesiae unitate*, 6, 7.

[2]Attributed to Athanasius, *De incarnatione et contra Arianos*, as cited in J. N. D. Kelley, *Early Christian Doctrines*, rev. ed. (New York: Harper & Row, 1978), 352.

[3]E. C. Miller, Jr., *Toward a Fuller Vision* (Wilton, CT: Morehouse-Barlow, 1984), 29.

[4]Richard Hooker, *Laws of Ecclesiastical Polity*, Book V, lvi, 13.

[5]F. D. Maurice, *The Kingdom of Christ*, ed. Alec R. Vidler, 2 vols., (London: SCM Press, 1958), 2:363.

[6]F. D. Maurice, *Theological Essays* (New York: Harper, 1957), 276-277.

Mission and Ecumenism: Together Not Apart

J. Robert Wright

First, it is a pleasure in this conference to honor the memory and the influence of Jackson Kemper, the Church's first missionary bishop, whose labors did so much to foster the concepts of the Episcopate as a missionary office and of Baptism as a missionary vocation given to all Christians.

Second, it is a pleasure to pay tribute in this conference today to our beloved Primate and Presiding Bishop, John M. Allin, whose twelve-year tenure as chief pastor of this Church may well be cited and celebrated by future historians for its bold and creative ventures in mission and renewal. When we think of the bishop as chief missionary, we think today above all of Bishop Allin, and we thank him for his initiatives in missionary and ecumenical leadership.

The subject assigned to me for this conference is "Ecumenism and Mission: Together Not Apart," and by way of introduction I want now to say a few words about the person recently elected to be our next Presiding Bishop, Edmond L. Browning, whom I think I have never met but for whom we all pray and about whom I have read much in the press over the last few weeks. Recently I was telephoned and interviewed for about two hours by a nationwide church publication related to another church, whose slightly devious reporter was trying to construct a future story to show that the election of Bishop Browning signalled an intention by the Episcopal Church to move away from its present ecumenical directions, at both poles so to speak, especially with the Roman Catholic and Lutheran churches, since the initial interviews of the Presiding Bishop-elect, as reported by the secular press, had not emphasized ecumenism and had instead seemed to focus upon an espousal of issues and causes and positions rather contrary to those formally held by the churches we generally regard as our closest ecumenical friends. As an Episcopal theologian and historian active in other ecumenical relations both nationally and internationally I was asked for my comment! Thanks a lot, I thought!

What I replied was this: Beyond the fact that I do not know the Presiding Bishop-elect personally, and hence do not really know what he does think about ecumenism, and the fact that the secular press reports often seem to err or mis-emphasize or mis-interpret or draw the wrong conclusions in religious reporting anyway, and the fact that our Presiding Bishop, whatever he may think or say, has less authority to bind the Episcopal Church than is the case with either the bishop of Rome for the Roman Catholic Church or even the Presiding Bishop of the Lutheran Church in America— apart from and in addition to those facts, I doubted very seriously if Presiding Bishop-Elect Browning would be opposed to ecumenism, and in fact I suspected he would really want to emphasize it, precisely because of his known commitment to mission and his past experience in Okinawa, Europe, and Hawaii, as executive for national and world mission at 815, and as the chairman of the Standing Commission on World Mission of the Episcopal Church. Ecumenism and mission, I said, echoing unintentionally my title for this paper, are in the Episcopal Church, and in Anglican theology generally, always held together, not apart, and our constant and consistent ecumenical policy has been to see ecumenism as a subservient but necessary adjunct to the mission of the church. To the Episcopal Church ecumenism is not an end in itself but rather for the sake of mission, I thus concluded my telephone interview, and it would therefore be theologically and practically inconsistent for any bishop who hoped to lead the Episcopal Church to emphasize but not to favor for that very reason closer ecumenical ties with other churches. Whatever the secular press, such as *Time Magazine* and the *New York Times* may have initially reported about the so-called "liberal activism" of the Presiding Bishop-elect (and the danger of misinterpretation must be watched in every press interview), I myself could give no credence to a conclusion that he would therefore be inclined to lead us in a direction away from our past and present ecumenical relations and commitments. In fact, I added, since we are now in a period in which the Roman Catholic leadership is widely perceived (whether correctly or not) as retreating from its earlier period of ecumenical initiative since the Second Vatican Council, it seems logical to expect our new Presiding Bishop to take a more aggressive stand and thus to resume once again the ecumenical leadership that characterized our Anglican involvement for so many long decades prior to Vatican II. Time will tell, of course, but Bishop Browning's initial press comments may possibly have been made with this in mind. If he favors mission, he must favor ecumenism!

And this, I am happy to say, although I had not yet at that time re-read it in preparation for this paper, is precisely the position that was approved and taken in print by the so-called Browning commission, the Standing Commission on World Mission of the General Convention of the Episcopal Church, which he then chaired, in its statement on "A Theology and Policy of Mission in Global Perspective" that was prepared for presentation to the General Convention of 1982 and endorsed by that convention. It is a specific emphasis of our present mission policy, the Browning report states, "to engage in joint action in mission with various Christian churches as a way of demonstrating our conviction that the thrusts toward mission and unity are not only compatible but inseparable."[1] "Mission and Ecumenism"—I can even retitle my paper from the report of this commission then chaired by Bishop Browning—are "not only compatible but inseparable"—that is, as my title does read, "together not apart." And please note the vital theological relationship between ecumenism and mission which this same report affirms:

Overcoming the scandal of division
Because it is the mission of the church to call all people to love God and live in a community that cuts across all human divisions, the Episcopal Church and all other churches of the Anglican Communion must not engage in mission in isolation from or with enmity toward Christians of other com-

munions. A divided church remains a great hindrance to mission. It presents a picture to the world not of love and peace but of strife and pride. As such, the common life of the church becomes a witness to the very thing it is supposed to stand against. It also makes it difficult for Christians to give each other the support and encouragement each owes to the other as they carry out the mission upon which they have all been sent. It is important to remember that the ecumenical movement was born out of the missionary movement and it is indeed mission that reminds us again and again that we are all to be one.

It is, therefore, disastrous to ignore the continuing divisions among Christians and the growing signs of indifference toward ecumenical relations. Discussion of world mission without a commitment to the unity of the church will prove to be a vacuous, perhaps even blasphemous, enterprise.[2]

And the slightly revised policy statement of this same commission that was accepted by the 1985 General Convention stipulated: "As new provinces are being formed and new ecumenical possibilities are developing, a renewed commitment to ecumenical dialogue and joint endeavors for both social renewal and evangelism needs to be made."[3]

Now it will be the purpose of this paper to do three things: first, to demonstrate and illustrate from my own research in the official publications of Lambeth Conferences, General Conventions, and the Anglican Consultative Council, that this same position, of mission and ecumenism as compatible and inseparable, together not apart, is anchored historically and theologically in official Anglican and Episcopal documents over a considerable period of time; second, to show how this position is developed and explicated as we see ecumenism at the service of mission from a selection of contemporary ecumenical documents in which we have some official investment; and third, to raise one difficult question, briefly, that this evidence presses upon us for the present and future. Each of these three sections of my paper will quote from the original sources, and each succeeding section will be shorter than its predecessor!

I

First we survey official Anglican documents to show that mission and ecumenism are intended to be held together, not apart. Most of the following excerpts come from a book which I have edited, *A Communion of Communions: One Eucharistic Fellowship.*[4]

1. Lambeth IV, 1897: Avoidance of Division in the Foreign Mission Field.

27. Resolved, That in the Foreign Mission Field of the Church's work, where signal spiritual blessings have attended the labours of Christian Missionaries not connected with the Anglican Communion, a special obligation has arisen to avoid, as far as possible without compromise of principle, whatever tends to prevent the due growth and manifestation of that "unity of the Spirit," which should ever mark the Church of Christ.

2. Lambeth V, 1908: Correlation and Co-operation of Missionary Agencies.

23. The Conference commends to the consideration of the Church the suggestions of the Committee on Foreign Missions, contained in their Report, for correlation and co-operation between Missions of the Anglican Communion and those of other Christian bodies.

3. Lambeth 1930: Statement of the nature and status of the Anglican Communion.

49. The Conference approves the following statement of the nature and status of the Anglican Communion. . . .

The Anglican Communion is a fellowship, within the One Holy Catholic and Apostolic Church, of those duly constituted Dioceses, Provinces or Regional Churches in communion with the See of Canterbury, which have the following characteristics in common:—

(a) they uphold and propagate the Catholic and Apostolic faith and order as they are generally set forth in the Book of Common Prayer as authorised in their several Churches;

(b) they are particular or national Churches, and, as such, promote within each of their territories a national expression of Christian faith, life and worship; and

(c) they are bound together not by a central legislative and executive authority, but by mutual loyalty sustained through the common counsel of the Bishops in conference.

The Conference makes this statement praying for and eagerly awaiting the time when the Churches of the present Anglican Communion will enter into communion with other parts of the Catholic Church not definable as Anglican in the above sense, as a step towards the ultimate reunion of all Christendom in one visibly united fellowship.

4. Lambeth IX, 1958: Statement on Christian Unity.

13. The Conference welcomes and endorses the Statement on Christian Unity contained in the Report of the Committee on Christianity and the Church Universal....

We believe that the mission of the Church is nothing less than the remaking and gathering together of the whole human race by incorporation into Christ. In obedience to this mission we must continually pray and work for the visible unity of all Christian believers of all races and nations in a living Christian fellowship of faith and sacrament, of love and prayer, witness and service.

The recovery and manifestation of unity, which we seek, is the unity of the whole Church of Christ. This means unity in living Christian fellowship, in obedience to Christ in every department of human life, and plain for all men to see. There can be no limit to the range of such unity. We are working for unity with the nonepiscopal Churches in our own countries and elsewhere. We continue to seek for such complete harmony of spirit and agreement in doctrine as would bring unity with the Eastern Orthodox Church and other ancient Churches. We must hope and pray for such eventual agreement in faith and order as shall lead to the healing of the breach between ourselves and the Church of Rome...

The unity between Christian Churches ought to be a living unity in the love of Christ which is shown in full Christian fellowship and in mutual service, while also, subject to sufficient agreement in faith and order, expressing itself in free interchange of ministries, and fullness of sacramental Communion. Such unity, while marked by the bond of the historic episcopate, should always include congregational fellowship, active participation both of clergy and laity in the mission and government of the Church, and zeal for evangelism.

Such is the vision we set before ourselves and our own people, calling them to regard the recovery and manifestation of the unity of the whole Church of Christ as a matter of the greatest urgency. We call upon our own Church members, under the leadership of the bishop and clergy of the diocese, in full loyalty to their own Church, to join with their fellow Christians in united prayer. And we urge them to do their utmost through national and local Councils for Churches, for common Christian witness and common service to their fellows. Only so can the world see the People of God giving united witness to the Lord Jesus Christ, and feeding, clothing, healing, and visiting the least of his brethren in his Name.

Finally we appeal to all our people to show a spirit of charity in their dealings with other Christians wherever they may be, to respect other Christian Churches, to refrain from harsh or unkind words about them, whether in speech or in writing, and to seek to understand both their life and their doctrine by common study and by personal contacts. Above all, we appeal to them to pray for Christian unity, privately, corporately, and together with members of other Christian communions, that all believers may be united "in the way Christ wills and by the means he chooses," and to remember always that the nearer we draw to Christ, the nearer we draw to one another.

5. Lambeth X, 1968: Anglican-Roman Catholic Relations.

52. The Conference welcomes the proposals made in the report of Section III which concern Anglican relations with the Roman Catholic Church. . . .

Together with the Roman Catholic Church we confess our faith in God, Father, Son, and Holy Spirit, as witnessed by the holy Scriptures, the Apostles' and Nicene Creeds, and by the teaching of the Fathers of the early Church. We have one baptism and recognize many common features in our heritage. At the same time substantial divergences exist, many of which have arisen since the sixteenth century, in such matters as the unity and indefectibility of the Church and its teaching authority, the Petrine primacy, infallibility, and Mariological definitions, as well as in some moral problems. These matters will require serious study so that they may be carefully identified and, under the guidance of the Spirit, resolved. This task must be undertaken in the light of the challenge to the whole Church of God presented by the modern world, and in the context of the mission of the Church throughout the world and to all sorts and conditions of men.

6. Lambeth X, 1968: Anglican Consultative Council: Functions.

3. To develop as far as possible agreed Anglican policies in the world mission of the Church and to encourage national and regional Churches to engage together in developing and implementing such policies by sharing their resources of manpower, money, and experience to the best advantage of all.

4. To keep before national and regional Churches the importance of the fullest possible Anglican collaboration with other Christian Churches.

5. To encourage and guide Anglican participation in the Ecumenical Movement and the ecumenical organizations; to co-operate with the World Council of Churches and the world confessional bodies on behalf of the Anglican Communion; and to make arrangements for the conduct of pan-Anglican conversations with the Roman Catholic Church, the Orthodox Churches, and other Churches.

7. General Convention, 1979: Resolution on the Nature of the Unity We Seek.

The visible unity we seek will be one eucharistic fellowship. As an expression of and a means toward this goal, the uniting Church will recognize itself as a communion of Communions, based upon acknowledgment of catholicity and apostolicity. In this organic relationship all will recognize each *other's members and ministries. All will share the bread and the cup of the Lord. All will acknowledge each other as belonging to the Body of Christ at all places and at all times. All will proclaim the Gospel to the world with one mind and purpose. All will serve the needs of humankind with mutual trust and dedication. And for these ends all will plan and decide together in assemblies constituted by authorized representatives whenever and wherever there is need.*

We do not yet see the shape of that collegiality, conciliarity, authority and primacy which need to be present and active in the Diocese with its Parishes as well as nationally, regionally, universally; but we recognize that some ecclesial structure will be necessary to bring about the expressions of our unity in the Body of Christ described above.

8. Ecumenical Report of the Executive Council of the Episcopal Church in the USA, 1979.

Ecumenism, with its emphasis on visible unity, is an essential part of the whole mission of the Church. "The mission of the Church is to restore all people to unity with God and each other in Christ" (Proposed Book of Common Prayer). The unity we have enables us to help strengthen Christians of other churches in their mission and be helped in return. A serious problem is that linkages between the churches are still weak. If we ask what should be different about the Episcopal Church's relations with other churches in the U.S. and throughout the world in future, the answer is networks.

It is essential to maintain and develop national, regional, world, and local ecumenical networks among families of churches (a) through existing ecumenical structures and, where they cannot or will not do the job, (b) through direct church-to-church relationships, so that "sustained and sustaining" relationships may increase. Churches may not delegate ecumenism to their ecumenical structures or to programs owned by those structures. The future task of the ecumenical structures is rather to enable conversation, planning, and communication among the churches.

9. Joint Agreed Statement of the Ecumenical Officers of the Churches of the Anglican Communion, 1981.

Theological dialogue however essential as a stage in the growth towards unity is not an end in itself. Its aim is to remove the obstacles our inherited divisions place in the way of the People of God uniting in mission. (The aim is to) transform the Churches' mission from a competitive drive to win members for our separate communities into a united action bringing the healing and reconciling power of the gospel to individuals and a divided society. This will reshape the existing Churches into forms more effective for this mission.

10. Anglican Consultative Council, 1981: Section 2 on "Unity and Ecumenical Affairs."

We believe it is an essential part of the Church's mission to strive for the unity of mankind, on the basis of principles grounded in natural justice proper to man, and elevated to the demands of divine charity by the truths of the gospel. The Church's mission, in a world of mounting uncertainty, is weakened by our lack of unity, leading to a loss both of corporate witness and of full personal formation and commitment in the life of the Church. By striving for the unity of the Church, we serve the unity of mankind.

II

If mission and ecumenism as compatible and inseparable, together not apart, is a position anchored historically and theologically in official Anglican and Episcopal policy documents, in this second section I want to show how this position is developed and explicated in a brief selection of some of our contemporary ecumenical documents. Here, in a way that is both direct and theological, we can see ecumenism at the service of the church's mission.

The first selection consists of excerpts from the "Agreed Statement on the Purpose or Mission of the Church," which was prepared by the officially appointed National Anglican-Roman Catholic Consultation in the USA and endorsed by the 1979 General Convention as "a description of the mandate this church has received to proclaim the Gospel of Our Lord Jesus Christ." This statement early reminds us that the church "is a community created and called by God. Its task is evangelization and salvation: to be an instrument of God's work in the world focused in the saving and liberating mission of Jesus Christ. It must, therefore, look to him for the example and style of its mission and to the Holy Spirit for the power to accomplish it."[5]

Next the statement develops its explication of the church's mission around the classical theme of the three-fold work of Christ as prophet, priest, and king, a theme that goes back to the writers of the early church, continues in those of the Middle Ages and Reformation, and can more recently be found no less than twenty-three times in the documents of Vatican Council II as well as in the 1968 Lambeth Conference and the 1979 American Book of Common Prayer. The mission of the whole church, both clergy and laity, in this statement's understanding, is the same as the mission or work of Christ himself: "The proclamation of the Good News, the praise of God's Name, and service to all people."[6] Such a definition is basically the same as that of the Catechism in our Book of Common Prayer: "to restore all people to unity with God and each other in Christ" as the church "prays and worships, proclaims the Gospel, and promotes justice, peace and love."[7] In such an understanding, therefore, the church's mission is everything the church does, or should be doing, in extending the reconciling work of Christ. Worship is one part of mission, and so is evangelism; church growth is one hoped-for result of evangelism.

But there are other definitions of mission that claim some following, and it may be instructive to review three of them here before we proceed to review the ARC statement. The first alternative definition, now largely discarded in the Episcopal Church in the USA, is to say that mission is all *non-self-supporting* work of the Church; this regretfully puts the definition on a financial basis. A second alternative is to define mission as all *humanward* work of the church, thus separating worship, which is Godward, from mission. And a third view, which has problems once it is defined, is to say that mission is everything the Church does or should do *only* with regard to persons and places to whom and where the Gospel has not yet been proclaimed.

Now we return to the ARC statement, and I select three quotes from it to show each point of its triad of proclamation, worship, and service:

The first thing the Church should be doing here and now is proclaiming the Gospel. The original Gospel was not only a message preached but also a life lived, and for this reason our proclamation today must involve not only preaching in words but also witness in deeds. The Church proclaims Jesus as Lord and Savior, both in its preaching and in its witness, and the response it asks is a following in both word and deed. The task of proclamation and likewise the necessity of response, moreover, are an obligation not only for individuals but also for the Church as a whole.[8]

The Church which proclaims God's Word expresses its own life most fully when it gathers as a community for worship, especially the celebration of the Eucharist, which is the summit and source of its mission. Worship, indeed, is part of the mission of the Church, for it testifies to the dependence of all people upon God and it affirms God's action for humanity in the death and resurrection of Jesus Christ, in the promise of the gift of the Spirit, and in our ultimate destiny of union with the Father.[9]

The imperative of viewing the Church's purpose in the context of "Service" (diakonia) has deep roots both in Holy Scripture and in the documents of our respective traditions. While this call to serve others and to place our resources at the service of others is recognized and widely discussed in each of our churches, we must confess that it does not appear that either of us has yet found the means to carry out this aspect of mission as successfully as we might. This presents a particular problem as well as a special opportunity to those Church members who find themselves among the affluent, for they possess, under God, particular means whereby the Church may become more fully a servant people, a sign of hope on mankind's way. One of the major challenges facing our churches is the cultivation of an awareness of "unjust systems and structures" that oppress human freedom, maintain situations of gross inequality, and facilitate individual selfishness. Forms of Christian service which do not take these structures into account are not adequate for the complexities of our day.[10]

And now some excerpts from the conclusion of this very fine statement:

The Church, the Body of Christ in the world, is led by the Spirit into all nations to fulfill the purpose of the Father. Insofar as it faithfully preaches the Gospel of salvation, celebrates the sacraments, and manifests the love of God in service, the Church becomes more perfectly one with the risen Christ. Impelled by its Lord, it strives to carry out the mission it has received from him: to prepare already the structures of the Kingdom, to share with all persons the hope for union with God.[11]

In humility and repentance, the Church shares the guilt of mankind in its disunity. Presenting men and women with hope in the fulfillment of their destiny beyond this life, it also assumes, under the cross of its Lord, the burdens and the struggles of the oppressed, the poor, and the suffering. Striving for justice and peace, the Church seeks to better the conditions of the world. To the divided, it offers oneness; to the oppressed, liberation; to the sick, healing; to the dying, life; to all persons, eternal salvation.[12]

We, as Roman Catholics and Episcopalians, charged by our churches to explore the possibility that there is a fundamental unity between us, find that we are in substantial agreement about the purpose or mission of the Church as we have set it forth above. We have uncovered no essential points on which we differ. And we know, also, that insofar as the Church appears visibly divided, its purpose is obscured, its mission impeded, and its witness weakened. We yearn, therefore, for a restoration of the unity that will serve our common purpose. Listening to the signs of the times, we seek guidance from the Spirit, so that through our common witness all may acknowledge that Jesus is the Lord, to the glory of God the Father, and that, in this faith, all may have life and have it abundantly.[13]

The other ecumenical document I want to cite is the 1982 "Lima Statement" on Baptism, Eucharist, and Ministry of the Faith and Order Commission of the World Council of Churches, for which I represented the Episcopal Church and upon whose final drafting committee I represented the Anglican Communion. By way of introduction, in order to summarize the way in which Lima puts ecumenism at the service of mission, I want to quote from the Church of England's response to BEM:

> *Throughout the three sections of the Lima Text, the sacramental life of the Church is related to the vocation to mission. In baptism we are committed to a life of obedience and sent out into the world; in the eucharist we are strengthened and renewed by the power of the Spirit to act as servants of reconciliation in a divided world; and the ordained ministry is given to the Church to build up the ministry of the whole Church to the world. Thus throughout, the Lima Text reminds us that unity and mission belong together. The unity of the Church is not an end in itself but for the service of God and for mission to the world.*[14]

Now I turn to the Lima/BEM text itself, and offer the following excerpts in order to show how mission is considered ecumenically in this important agreement that has just been substantially endorsed by the 1985 General Convention. First, in relation to Baptism:

> *As the churches grow into unity, they are asking how their understandings and practices of baptism, eucharist and ministry relate to their mission in and for the renewal of human community as they seek to promote justice, peace and reconciliation. Therefore our understanding of these cannot be divorced from the redemptive and liberating mission of Christ through the churches in the modern world.*[15]

> *As they grow in the Christian life of faith, baptized believers demonstrate that humanity can be regenerated and liberated. They have a common responsibility, here and now, to bear witness together to the Gospel of Christ, the Liberator of all human beings. The context of this common witness is the Church and the world. Within a fellowship of witness and service, Christians discover the full significance of the one baptism as the gift of God to all God's people. Likewise, they acknowledge that baptism, as a baptism into Christ's death, has ethical implications which not only call for personal sanctification, but also motivate Christians to strive for the realization of the will of God in all realms of life (Rom.*

6:9ff; Gal. 3:27-28; 1 Peter 2:21—4:6).[16]

And then, mission in relation to the Eucharist:

The eucharistic celebration demands reconciliation and sharing among all those regarded as brothers and sisters in the one family of God and is a constant challenge in the search for appropriate relationships in social, economic and political life (Matt. 5:23f; I Cor. 10:16f; I Cor. 11:20-22; Gal. 3:28). All kinds of injustice, racism, separation and lack of freedom are radically challenged when we share in the body and blood of Christ. Through the eucharist the all-renewing grace of God penetrates and restores human personality and dignity. The eucharist involves the believer in the central event of the world's history. As participants in the eucharist, therefore, we prove inconsistent if we are not actively participating in this ongoing restoration of the world's situation and the human condition. The eucharist shows us that our behaviour is inconsistent in face of the reconciling presence of God in human history: we are placed under continual judgment by the persistence of unjust relationships of all kinds in our society, the manifold divisions on account of human pride, material interest and power politics and, above all, the obstinacy of unjustifiable confessional oppositions within the body of Christ.[17]

The eucharist is precious food for missionaries, bread and wine for pilgrims on their apostolic journey. The eucharistic community is nourished and strengthened for confessing by word and action the Lord Jesus Christ who gave his life for the salvation of the world. As it becomes one people, sharing the meal of the one Lord, the eucharistic assembly must be concerned for gathering also those who are at present beyond its visible limits, because Christ invited to his feast all for whom he died. Insofar as Christians cannot unite in full fellowship around the same table to eat the same loaf and drink from the same cup, their missionary witness is weakened at both the individual and the corporate levels.[18]

III

Our ecumenical relations and agreements are at the service of the church's mission, together not apart, but they do raise a problem. I conclude with one difficult question for the mission of the church that our ecumenical relations and dialogues are increasingly pressing upon us. It is the question of authority for the sake of mission. The official response of the Episcopal Church to the *Final Report* of the Anglican-Roman Catholic International Commission, which was voted at the General Convention that has just concluded (1985), raises the question, at first in a rather innocent way, of "the process of authority by which decisions about faith and action should be taken for the sake of the Church's mission."[19] The context is the discussion of papal infallibility in the *Final Report* of ARCIC I, in which the Anglican signatories to that report felt obliged to dissent from the Roman Catholic position. They stated, from a typical Anglican viewpoint, that if a papal definition proposed as infallible "were not manifestly a legitimate interpretation of biblical faith and in line with orthodox tradition, Anglicans would think it a duty to reserve the reception of the definition for study and discussion."[20] Well and good, but the query has been raised in reply, by no less than Cardinal Ratzinger of the Sacred Congregation but also by many Anglicans, how would we decide—by what authority—whether in the last analysis something is or is not "manifestly a legitimate interpretation of biblical faith"?[21] When there is a major controverted question about the church's mission—about what it should teach or do, how do we reach an authoritative and binding decision? Even when our own House of Bishops, or General Convention, votes and appears to decide a question of major controversy about the church's mission, how do we get them even to agree that they have reached an agreement? And of course even if there is a discernible position of the Episcopal Church in the USA, there may well be other churches of the Anglican Communion who hold, as they are presently entitled to do, very different positions about the same question. Even Lambeth Conference decisions by Anglican bishops, as we are reminded inside the front cover of every volume of them, have no binding authority unless they are accepted by the individual churches in each province.

What is, really, the Anglican position about such mission frontiers today as women's ordination, homosexuality, abortion, about Christology and the facticity of the Incarnation, about the arms race, about American government involvement in the third world, about the unequal distribution of the world's wealth, about any Christian mission to the Jews, about conversion of other religions, about which churches are entitled to the name "Anglican," about which liturgical usage should prevail in a given mission area, about overlapping Anglican jurisdictions overseas and whether Morning Prayer or the Eucharist is to be presented in any given mission as the central worship of the church, about whether we cooperate or not (and if so, in what ways) with which other churches in overseas missions, about whether there is to be any international coordination and direction of all our mission efforts, both among Anglicans from different home countries and with the missions of, say the Roman Catholic or Lutheran churches? And so on! It is relatively easy to agree that we should be a missionary church, but it is much more difficult to agree as to what we should do and teach as we go about our mission. Only a fool would conclude that we need no common policy, that it really doesn't matter, that we need not at least try to reach agreement about common answers to such questions as these, to articulate a mission to these parties, as Professor Griffiss might well have said it. Rank individualism is the only alternative, and to opt for it is to opt for unlimited confusion and weakened credibility especially in mission situations. Such comfortable pluralism may well be one reason why Anglicanism is so attractive to some people, but it clearly undercuts any larger unitary vision. As the Browning Report put it, "A divided church remains a great hindrance to mission. It presents a picture to the world not of love and peace but of strife and pride."

The *Final Report* of ARCIC I, as well as the reports coming from many other of our ecumenical dialogues today, as well as the pressing needs coming from actual mission situations, are all asking for us that we clarify and specify what we believe about the Christian faith, and what we should do in response to it, and that we frame our answers in relation to the positions of other churches with whom we hope to reach a common mind about God's will for the church's mission and a common strategy for effecting it. Thoughtless Anglicans sometimes boastfully claim that we are a non-confessional church, that nobody ever has to be de-programmed from the Episcopal Church, but when one really thinks about it this is not necessarily something to be so proud of—to claim that we have no program, nothing specific to confess in common but only a limitless pluralism open to everyone of every point of view or practice. The diversity, even ambiguity, of Anglican teaching and mission praxis around the world is astounding, as for example Stephen Sykes' book *The Integrity of Anglicanism* reminded us a few years ago, and other churches, our ecumenical partners, in dialogue now ask us: do we really want to be the church that tolerates everything? So the question of authority is upon us. I am raising it, not answering it here.

It was the 1979 General Convention's resolution on "The Nature of the Unity We Seek" which indicated that collegiality, conciliarity, authority, and primacy, on an ecumenical basis, will be needed in every parish, diocese, nation, and region, as well as universally, for the sake of the church's mission, and it is in the context of universal, worldwide mission that the ARCIC *Final Report* sets the question of universal authority—a subject now under discussion in other ecumenical dialogues as well. If we agree with its Anglican signatories in rejecting papal infallibility and unlimited papal jurisdiction and even its present exercise, must we also reject every kind of even limited papal primatial authority, such as the ARCIC *Final Report* argues for and such as the 1979 General Convention seemed to envisage and such as the 1985 General Convention has now cautiously foreseen as at least a possibility, when such a primatial authority is clearly conceived in pastoral terms for the service of the church's unity and mission? Do we have a better alternative, for the sake of the church's universal mission? Jackson Kemper was not called to be a missionary bishop by an already existing diocese; rather, he was sent to be a missionary bishop by a central authority, by the central authority appropriate to the national and regional limitations under which we then operated. But today, as Nelson Burr so eloquently noted, mission is everywhere, and we must think of it in global terms.

All churches do mission today in the light of the widespread scriptural, patristic, liturgical, and ecumenical renewals we now experience. I think the reaping of their results is one exciting characteristic of the period beginning in 1970, to use Roland Foster's helpful chronology, and the present Archbishop of Canterbury has called for ecumenical collaboration with other churches at every possible level because we know that "By ourselves we shall likely get it wrong." Ecumenism stands in the service of mission.

And so I conclude. If tomorrow we are to continue with our Presiding Bishop to venture in mission, and if we are to agree (and I do) with the Browning commission that mission and unity are not only compatible but inseparable, together not apart, then we are going to need some sort of visible worldwide authority in the church that can somehow face and meet the questions that arise in the expanding global situation that lies ahead. The problem is: how to articulate and pursue an authoritatively coherent mission on every frontier that we face. Our bishops in particular are charged to boldly proclaim and interpret the Gospel, to guard the faith, unity, and discipline, and with their fellow bishops to share in the leadership of the church throughout the world. If they are the ones to lead us in mission strategy now, they must lead us in facing the ecumenical problem of authority. May we dare to hope that this will be one priority (among many) for our new Presiding Bishop?

End Notes

[1]*Mission in Global Perspective* (Cincinnati: Forward Movement Publications, 1982), 35.

[2]Ibid., 27-28.

[3]"Report of The Standing Committee on World Mission," in *The Blue Book: Reports of the Committees, Commissions, Boards, and Agencies of The General Convention of the Episcopal Church, Los Angeles, California, September 1985*, 330.

[4]J. Robert Wright, ed., *A Communion of Communions: One Eucharistic Fellowship* (New York: The Seabury Press, 1979).

[5]ARC, "Agreed Statement on the Purpose or Mission of the Church," para. 7, in *Ecumenical Trends* 5 (January 1976): 4 (hereafter cited ASPMC).

[6]ASPMC, para. 8, 4.

[7]*The Book of Common Prayer* (New York: Church Hymnal Corp., 1979), 855.

[8]ASPMC, para. 10, 5.

[9]Ibid., para. 12, 6.

[10]Ibid, para. 14, 7.

[11]Ibid., para. 17, 8.

[12]Ibid., para. 18, 8.

[13]Ibid., para. 19, 9.

[14]*Towards a Church of England Response to BEM and ARCIC* (London: CIO Publishing, 1985), 47.

[15]*Baptism, Eucharist and Ministry,* Faith and Order Paper 111 (Geneva: World Council of Churches, 1982), Preface, viii-ix (hereafter cited *BEM*).

[16]*BEM*, Baptism, para. 10, 4.

[17]Ibid., Eucharist, para. 20, 14.

[18]Ibid., para. 26, 15.

[19]"Report of the Standing Commission on Ecumenical Relations on the ARCIC Final Report," in *The Blue Book*, 40.

[20]ARCIC, "Authority in the Church II," para. 29, in *The Final Report: Anglican-Roman Catholic International Commission* (Cincinnati: Forward Movement Publications, 1982; Washington, D.C.: Office of Publishing Services, U.S. Catholic Conference, 1982), 95.

[21]See Joseph Ratzinger, "Anglican-Catholic Dialogue: Its Problems and Hopes," *Insight* 1(March 1983): 2-11.

A Vision of Mission

John Maury Allin

To contemplate and reflect a vision of the Christian mission within the particular context of a celebration of the life and offering of Jackson Kemper, during the 150th anniversary of his consecration as an apostolic servant in and of the Christian mission, is to share a perspective from the past with an unlimited view of the future. Bishop Kemper was called to extend the Church's mission on the expanding frontier of this then new nation on the vast North American continent. The viewpoint we can share with him is enlightened by compelling evangelistic faith. Jackson Kemper embodied both the Christian message and mission.

In thinking of mission and ministry, the familiar missionary text recorded in verses 35 through 38 of the 9th chapter of the Gospel according to St. Matthew are remembered:

And Jesus went about all the cities and villages, teaching in their synagogues, and preaching the gospel of the kingdom, and healing every sickness and every disease among the people. But when he saw the multitudes, he was moved with compassion on them, because they fainted, and were scattered abroad, as sheep having no shepherd. Then saith he unto his disciples, the harvest truly is plenteous, but the laborers are few; Pray ye therefore the Lord of the harvest, that he will send forth laborers into his harvest.

There is clear indication that Jackson Kemper received and responded to those words of our Lord Jesus. They express the vocation Kemper heeded and obeyed. Standing in the middle of this vast and expansive land, one can envision a newly consecrated vigorous bishop, standing by a rail fence alongside a field of abundant grain, looking westward. There is evidence Jackson Kemper had the ability to look over the fences and other obstacles which separated him from the

117

fields to be harvested and saw the harvest spread toward a horizon marking the infinite reaches of eternity.

There is also evidence that Bishop Kemper knew how to climb over or get through fences and other barriers to mission. He well understood that progress in the Christian mission, as in any journey toward any goal, depended on the direction and confidence of the next step. One likes to think of any Christian missionary as having confidence enough to take the next step because of the faith that the journey has infinite possibilities. And the infinite possibilities are set forth in the Christian Gospel message, the Word of that message being the generating power of the mission we Christians share with Jackson Kemper.

The mission of the Church has moved forward in time and space like meandering rivers upon which many early missionaries traveled and crossed, bearing the Word. Borrowing from the imagery of Holy Scripture, the flowing forth of the Gospel stream becomes for many "the river whose streams make glad the city of God" and can make the "desert bloom like the rose" (Ps. 46:4; Isa. 35:1).

To get to the heart of the issue is to turn in the Christian faith to the source of life and light. Only in the Christ light is there vision of the mission for life, the more abundant life meant to be shared by all with the loving source of life. However, the harsh reality is that many evil misdirected forces move to interfere and overshadow the light and the truth and justice of love in life. The truth is that often Church members have lost the way in Christian mission because they lost or moved away from the light. No light, no vision, and goals and purposes become blurred, distorted, and directions reversed.

Prerequisite to being messengers on Christian mission is to have the message. An accurate vision of Christian mission includes not only the multitudes unreached, those unrelated to the fulfilling life—and caught in life-draining conditions, but also the many who were reached by Church agents or agencies yet never received the life of the message or a clear vision of the Christian mission. How widely the responsibility or irresponsibility for this failure extends among us, whose vocation, occupation, commitment and engagement is the Christian mission is a question concerning all of the baptized. It is a primary cause for self-examination. And that is a basic exercise in Christian mission.

A clear view of Christian mission comes with a clear view of Jesus Christ. How clear is your view of Jesus Christ and his mission? That is a direct question we Christians need to answer frequently and accurately. Thus "disciple" and "discipleship" become active descriptions and not archaic terms. In Christian faith discipline becomes a graceful way of life rather than an expression of punishment. The Christian mission depends upon disciplined missionaries.

Let me repeat and record here some words addressed by the Presiding Bishop to the 68th General Convention of the Episcopal Church in 1985:

> *The blunt truth is there are many nominal members of this Church who have yet to be led to learning and sharing the experience of Christian mission. Many members of the Church participate by proxy. They have little understanding of Christian faith or the missionary purpose of Christ's Church. Their participation in Church life is limited to baptisms, marriages and burials. Many would happily authorize proxies for these events if such could be arranged.*

> *Membership in the faith community of the Christian Church logically and theologically is expected to be an affirmation that Jesus of Nazareth is Christ the Lord. To each member of this Church is addressed the question: "What think ye of Christ?" Some have yet to answer.*

> *Is Jesus the only-begotten Son of God? Is his Gospel to be preached to all nations and to the uttermost? Did Jesus offer his life for all or just those chosen for Church membership?*

> *Are faith and repentence still requirements for baptism and church membership, or does one merely have to agree to associate occasionally with some designated Christians?*

> *What think ye of Christ, brothers and sisters? Is he the Saviour of the world? Do others experience the love of God in Jesus Christ as a result of our efforts? Is Jesus the one who was to come, or do we look for another?*

Not every Christian is skilled in preaching the Gospel. Yet every Christian can know the Gospel, keep the Lord's company, tell the Lord's story, serve in the Lord's spirit, and be moved by his love to love others.

This, brothers and sisters, is the *raison d'etre* of our Christian mission, and if not, then we are here under an assumed name.

Here let me plainly profess and share my faith: The mission of Jesus Christ is for truth and justice, for reconciliation, for peace and the fulfillment of the good purpose of the holy Creator. I share the faith that the nature and being of the only Creator is holy love. I believe that holy love is most effectively made manifest in Jesus of Nazareth. In faith and profession I believe Jesus is the Christ, the only-begotten of God, full of grace and truth. I believe the experience of the Christ comes through this Jesus of history.

The vision of mission in this world today is blurred, reflecting uncertainty. There is concern for righteousness, justice, human well-being in the Church. There is desire for better living conditions in the world, more equitable distribution of earth's resources, hope for better life with the possibility of continuing beyond death. Yet the vision of mission among Christians has become limited, fragmented, even provincial. For many the view ends at the horizon. There is need among Christians now to refocus, clarify and enlarge our missionary perspective. The Church's company is halted and divided between two opinions. Is there one Lord, one faith, one God and Father of all with one comprehensive mission to the whole world, or many? Is Jesus Christ the Lord or one among the prophets?

In our contemporary Christian terminology the word "fundamentalism" is given the definition of "literalism." The interpretation is a simplistic belief in the Holy Scriptures. Between the literal and the liberal interpretations of the Gospel message the fundamentals of Christian faith and mission are often confused, compromised, confounded. Reaction to "literalism" tends to redefine words, overshadows their radical meaning, questions their transmission and makes Gospel imperatives optional. Both "literalism" and "liberalism" paradoxically can become more concerned with proof or disproof of dogma than with the free response of faith. And so the vision of Christian mission becomes blurred with blind spots, appearing like a mosaic with central pieces missing. Is our song and purpose to bring the world to Christ, or did that idea and hymn pass with the Victorian age?

My vision of the Christian mission is of all baptized and engrafted into the mystical body of Christ engaged in the endeavor to relate all life in the love of God through the sacrifice of Jesus Christ. With continuing repentance for evil or erroneous practices in the Church's history, the vision of the Christian process is to reach and relate the peoples of earth to God through Christ by loving service, the witness of worship, sharing the search for truth in sharing the good news and life of the Gospel. I envision a graceful company with common faith offering life to others, all sorts and conditions of other human beings, recognizing the uniqueness and heritage of each and striving to protect their freedom of choice, that essential of the gift of love. Though the Church, through human frailty, be reduced to a remnant, I envision that remnant in mission with a loving ministry free from claims of super or dominant righteousness. Though the vocation to Christian mission is to an overwhelming task, I believe God will continue to raise up those who can respond in the faith and knowledge that the mission cannot be accomplished by the accumulation of good works, but ever depends upon the grace of God.

Paul of Tarsus continues, as we now say, a "state of the art" model of missionary. The two contrasting examples of the methods and missions in Paul's life are clear lessons for our vision of mission. To be avoided in the Christian mission is the model and method of Saul the Pharisee in his mission to seek out and purge the Christians from the religion that had formed him. Delegated authority, arrest, coercion and force were his instruments. The useful perspective for our vision of mission continues to be Paul of Tarsus, faithful servant, evangelist, teacher, with artisan skills to earn his own passage or livelihood where needed. He offered what he had and who he was in the name, grace and service of his Lord. While Christians have learned much since

Paul's age, his vision of the Lord, the responsibility of his faith and the spirit and quality of his self-offering provide a clear focus for the vision of Christian mission.

So the mosaic of mission emerges with the addition of a brilliant Paul, a confidently responsive Kemper, and with room for the likes of you or me.

The Christian vision of mission is one of endless opportunity to those who believe and serve the Lord.

Sermon at the Opening Eucharist:
for Jackson Kemper

Roger John White

> *The Lord called me from the womb. . . . And he said to me,*
> *"You are my servant. . . . I will give you as a light to the*
> *nations, that my salvation may reach to the end of the earth."*
> *(Isa. 49:1-6)*

We have come together to give thanks for the life of one of God's servants: a man called, convinced of God's abiding presence and power, and commissioned to be the conveyor of light and hope, sustained in the knowledge that salvation was his and available to all through Jesus Christ, his Lord and Savior.

It is a great privilege to be called to be one who follows in the footsteps of this servant of God. May we open our hearts and minds to the spirit of this first missionary bishop of our Church; may we learn of him and allow his example to frame our mission and ministry, sharing his basic promise that with God all things are possible.

Let me begin at the end of his life, for I believe the essence of his life as servant—evangelist—missionary—is to be found in some of his last words:

> *I have everything to be thankful for; the presence of my*
> *Saviour, the help of His Holy Spirit, and a hope full of*
> *immortality.*

Jackson Kemper responded with joy to his call to servanthood. He was convinced that God and only God could fulfill his mission through the help of servants filled with the power and presence of the Holy Spirit. This faith permeated his life, his mission and ministry. It gave him the strong hope of salvation, and he could only respond with deep and sincere thankfulness for God's love and mercy which had been poured upon him. What simple straightforward gifts Jackson possessed. We are told:

He overflowed with the joy of thanksgiving. He knew the presence of the Holy Spirit. He was convinced of the power of the Holy Spirit working through him and he framed his missionary methods accordingly. He lived his life with a sure hope before him.

Who was this servant called by God to spread His light, to proclaim salvation to what then seemed to be the end of the earth? He was, in the words of St. Paul, "one of God's fellow workers"; one who knew that "the foundation on which he built was Jesus Christ himself." Jackson acknowledged that it was Christ who would continue to build on that foundation through his "called servants."

Jackson Kemper was from all accounts a man with a childlike cheerfulness and an absorbing sense of duty to serve his Lord. He knew where he was going, what he was called to do, and went about it with order, strategy, enthusiasm and a clear methodology. He was described as a person "whose greatest mission was the Church" and its mission. Another tells us that he had "a calm devotion to duty which is perhaps the most typical Anglican form of Christian character."

Kemper's own watchwords—"Evangelical Truth and Apostolic Order"—allow us to see the faith and driving force of this missionary bishop. He was a proclaimer of the Good News of God in Christ and a believer that in the Church, God had called together fellow workers to serve their Lord in mission as we hear in the Gospel of Matthew:

Go therefore and make disciples of all nations, baptizing them in the name of the Father and of the Son and of the Holy Spirit, teaching them to observe all that I have commanded you; and lo, I am with you always, to the close of the age. (Matt. 28:19-20)

Such evangelical proclamation and apostolic methodology were combined with incredible drive, enthusiasm and stamina in our first missionary bishop. Bishop Daniel Tuttle of Missouri, writing with a great sense of joy, jubilation and friendship about Kemper, said: "It was doing and smiling that he had time for," and "Cheerily he did his part to CALL OUT and SEND FORTH."

What clarity of mission strategy we find embedded here! A bishop courageous enough to challenge his people and call out from their midst proclaimers of the Word to be sent forth to baptize and to spread light to the world.

"Never did he ask of others," it is said, "what he did not exemplify himself." He believed in leading, being the spearhead of mission and being the example for others of servanthood in the Lord. It was this man who with great reluctance gave up being a missionary bishop, a title he cherished, to become the first diocesan of Wisconsin.

He was convinced that a successor to the apostles was to be the spearhead of missionary work, not the maintainer of the Church. Others could be called out and join him to be sent forth, and others could build up the flock as the mission went forward. But for Jackson Kemper the bishop was a missionary—out of the office and into the forefront of mission "building up," and then releasing his oversight to others.

Listen to the Bishop of Eau Claire, Frank Wilson, who wrote in 1935: "Kemper's missionary policy was to build up sufficient church strength in a given state to carry itself as a diocese and then to release it from his jurisdiction to make its way under its own bishop." Another chronicler says that the central aim of his office as missionary bishop was "to supervise and encourage the formation of parishes."

I would contend that such strategy requires a strong conviction that it is God who fulfills the mission of the Church and that we are fellow workers. We need faith enough to plant, build up and release, allowing God then to work through others to enable the message of salvation to spread.

For bishops today, Jackson's example points to episcopal leadership in mission strategy and the implementation of strategy. It points to bishops who are capable of being enablers of others so that the Holy Spirit can be found to walk in and through those called out and sent forth, and then released to permit God to work through their lives using their particular gifts.

The message also for the episcopate is that it helps to be an optimist. "Kemper was convinced," we are told, "that if people would practice their Christian principles and follow along the way which the Church pointed out to them, all problems would be automatically solved." He believed that God could work through what he had created in human form if God were permitted to shine through problems.

Jackson did not always maintain such optimism. In 1853 he said, "I have almost thought at times I commanded the forlorn hope." Here we see, though, an indication of his saintliness and humanness. He was, said Bishop Tuttle, a man with no airs, simple, sensible, practical, straightforward, active, energetic, and earnest. Almost always cheery, he was a gentleman who showed courtesy to all and projected hope in all that he did. These God-given earthy gifts allowed this man to win hearts, and then through Christ to save souls and to build up the Church with evangelical zeal while maintaining apostolic order—gifts still needed by all missionaries, and especially by bishops.

Kemper had little time or enthusiasm for "in-house" Church controversy, a lesson we have still to learn. He was convinced that such controversy was detrimental to the preaching of Christ's Gospel and took vital energy away from the life of his Church, for internal turmoil distracts from our baptismal call to proclaim, teach, preach, and heal.

Such "in-house" squabbling consumes us and distracts our vision, our energy and renders us impotent in our calling as servants, as missionaries. If the Church is the means through which God can fulfill his mission, we will need all our energy and direction focused toward that goal alone. Such clear priorities in the life and mission of the Church, together with energy, cheerfulness and hope can be the means whereby we move from our maintenance stance as a Church and rekindle the spirit of Kemper, and once again become filled with evangelical zeal and clarity of mission.

Jackson Kemper's concept of mission clearly put the different aspects of Church life in order of priority. He found parishes and institutions such as Nashotah House in order to forward the mission of the Church. They were not foundations created for the glory of the Church or themselves, but to further better the Church as servant, to build up the Church for mission and ministry so that the Church could be used up in Christ's witness and service in the world. Kemper's foundations were support mechanisms for mission and never intended to be self-serving, but only for the glory of God.

We need to reappraise our priorities in the life of the Church. Do our resources, our manpower, our strategy in the life of the Church enhance, support and further its true mission? Or are they shackles holding us back from seeing the vision of our mission and its fulfillment in and through this body called to be servant?

Jackson Kemper knew that Christ was with him and had given him new life and hope. That has to be *first*. Only then can we respond and begin to fulfill our call to go out and make disciples and preach the Gospel in word and deed, bringing others to know our Lord and Savior, and enabling them through their life in the Church to be human, yes, but also enthused, built up and supported and then released.

It has been my intent to hold up before you this saintly, human, zealous servant called Jackson. I hold him up so that we may "drink in" his enthusiasm for Christ's mission. I hold him up before you that bishops may catch his clarity of direction and leadership. I hold him up before the Church as an example of God working in and through this servant to bring great fruitfulness in mission.

Kemper's example offers to all of us who would minister for Christ the opportunity to set a clear strategy, to examine our stewardship of gifts and money as we prioritize their use in the mission of the Church. It offers a need for the Body of Christ to examine how it calls out those who are to be in Orders to lead, enable, enthuse and encourage the whole Body in its mission of hope to a wearied and splintering world. His example poses before all of us the issue of the use of Church institutions and staff, demanding us to ask whether they are servants and support mechanisms for the furtherance of Christ's mission or factors which work against the concept of servanthood in our preaching, teaching and healing in this world.

May these few days change your life as you meet this servant "called from the womb" to spread the light of Christ. May you learn from him to respond to the Gospel with deep gratitude. May you come to know Christ as the very center of your living as he did. May you open your heart, life and ministry and allow God through the Holy Spirit to work through you. May you be so refreshed and renewed that you live as though you have hope of eternal life and overflow with such joy that others come to share that hope.

I leave with you the commission given to Jackson Kemper by Bishop Doane of New Jersey in 1835. I hope you will make it your own.

> *Beloved, go! Go, bear, before a ruined world, the Saviour's bleeding Cross. Go, feed, with bread from heaven, the Saviour's hungering Church. Go, thrice beloved, go and God the Lord go with you!*

And so Jackson went and did. Will we? With equal evangelical zeal for the truth of Christ?

Sermon at the Eucharist:
for the Mission of the Church

Arthur A. Vogel

After this the Lord appointed seventy others, and sent them on ahead of him, two by two, into every town and place where he himself was about to come.

(Luke 10:1)

The mission of the Church needs invigoration.

The growth of the early Church is frequently used as proof that the Spirit of God dwelt in it and led it. The Spirit of God dwells in and leads the Church now, and certainly the Church has grown over its 2,000 year history.

The Church is growing some places now, most notably in Africa, but the Church appears not to be growing where it was first planted—where it first spread—in the West. The Church is not growing where it is the oldest.

Having said that, we must pause a moment to ask whether or not, if the Church is itself, it can become old? Can it become old if it bears witness to a God who makes all things new?

The mission of the Church needs invigoration.

Where can we find the answer to the Church's needs? The Episcopal Church nationally, and in almost all of its dioceses, has turned to activities in evangelism and renewal for the answer. We have a national evangelism officer, and I am sure that your diocese, as mine, has a department or commission of evangelism and renewal.

I still think the best definition of "evangelism" is "good-news-ism." Everything Christian is good news.

I have said hundreds of times and probably thousands of times—and you have heard or said hundreds of times, probably thousands of times—that good news cannot be kept secret. If something good happens to you, others will know about it. If you unexpectedly inherit a million dollars, you will share the news with others, and if you are in love, everyone will know. As bad as we are at keeping our troubles to ourselves, we are even worse at keeping good news to ourselves!

But as true as the principle is that good news must be shared, is it helping?

As we encourage people through our emphasis on evangelism and renewal to spread the Good News, too much emphasis appears to fall on our personal feelings. If we are pleased, we spread the Good News. We may keep it to ourselves, or take just enough of it to get us through our difficult days. We turn the Good News into good news for us; we can be very existential about it.

One of the saddest duties which befalls a bishop is to deconsecrate a church. That sad duty befell me within the last year. I had to go to a pleasant, small north-central Missouri town and deconsecrate one of the most beautiful and well situated church buildings in our entire diocese. The building needed basic structural repairs if it was to remain safely in use; estimates ranged from $12,000 to $15,000 for the work; and we had but three regular and active communicants in the congregation. It would have been immoral to spend our limited resources in such quantity for so few people.

After the priest I took with me as witness and I left the church at the conclusion of the brief service, we stopped at the home of an elderly woman, who was one of our remaining communicants. She asked us to have lunch with her in a local restaurant, and, of course, we were pleased to accept her invitation. After lunch, when I had driven her back home, she asked if I would come in for just a moment and read something. She said it would only take a few moments and she had the material ready for me. As I walked into her living room I saw a book lying open, face down on a small coffee table. She handed it to me and explained that it had been written by a minister of another denomination in 1910 and that it was a history of the town up to that point in its life. The page and one-half open for me to read was a description of the Episcopal congregation at the church I had just deconsecrated.

I read that in the year 1900 the congregation at Grace Episcopal Church numbered 150 people, with 50 children in the church school. In 1985 three communicants were left, but other churches had been built in the meantime on the same square our church faced, and two of them could have contained our church building four or five times over.

Can the Good News be kept secret? What had happened?

We need an understanding of the Church's mission which rules out the possibility of selfishness—which rules out even the possibility of our feelings taking priority over the mission of the Church.

That is why speaking just of the mission of the Church will not do; mission needs to be qualified, specified as a certain kind of mission, if it is to be Christian mission.

We all know plenty of people who are on missions in the world. Some of them have goals for the Church, and some of them even have goals for God. As a matter of fact, "Goals for God" is a rather catchy slogan. I think we might be able to stir people with it; it would go well on television. I believe I know people who are already living their religion according to the slogan, "Goals for God." These people are doing something for God—they are doing what they are sure needs to be done for God in the world—and they are equally sure that, when they are finished, God will thank them and congratulate them for their work on his behalf. God will reward his friends, those who have worked for him, and their ultimate reward will be heaven.

Such people are good at setting their sights, homing in on a target, often reaching their goal. The goal may be Church growth.

Success!

But in the process mission has become a missile. Mission which is totally controlled by method, mission which is completely programmed, becomes a missile. Such a mission is impersonal, even if its goal is Church growth. Process controls everything.

Certainly it is true that one aspect of the mission of the Church is to grow. The Church is to grow by every means possible, but not by any means possible.

The mission of the Church must be understood in terms which rule out its mission being controlled by us. We—you and I, our egos—must be controlled by mission. Our feelings must not be decisive.

Spreading the Good News—evangelism—is a great idea, but the failure of the mission of the Church proves that we have found a way to appropriate the Good News to ourselves.

Can we, on the other hand, make such an appropriation with the concept "apostolic"? "Apostolic" means "being sent." The idea of "being sent" includes within itself reference to someone beyond us—the sender.

I suggest that the qualification to mission which we must always use in order to make the mission of the Church Christian is "apostolic." Christian mission is apostolic mission.

But having said that, we may ask whether any real advance has been made, for it could well be asked whether or not the statement, "Christian mission is apostolic mission," is a redundancy.

"Mission," from the Latin *missio*, means "sent." "Missile" comes from the same word and means "something sent," or "something hurled." "Missile" often meant "javelin." (I will refrain from saying that at least such a mission had a point to it.)

It is because of the impersonal and mechanistic nature of so many missions that we have to use another word for the same thing to have the proper meaning of Christian mission recognized. "Apostolic" is the word. When we hear or read the word "apostolic," do we not immediately think of the apostles, persons who were sent? The person, not the journey, is emphasized by "apostle," as over against the impersonal planning which may be used to accomplish a mission. As a matter of fact, many missions are best accomplished anonymously or impersonally. Some missions require work at midnight by people dressed in black so that they cannot be known.

I believe we should use "apostolic" as much as, and often more than or in place of, "evangelistic." Anglicans do not use "apostolic" enough.

Many years ago when I was teaching theology at Nashotah House, I met two Roman Catholic priests who were on the faculty of the diocesan seminary in Mundelein, Illinois. We found that we had a number of interests in common, and they invited me to come to their school for a visit. I was pleased to do so and was most cordially received by them. I met a number of their colleagues, toured the campus, and had a most delightful meal—the latter all by ourselves in a private dining room. The visit took place a number of years before Vatican II, and guests such as I were not permitted to eat with the students in those days. I discovered an excellent collection of Anglican theology on the top floor of their library—behind lock and key so that the students could not get at it. One of my hosts had a fine selection of Anglican authors on loan in his room, however, and I was glad to learn of his interest in us.

My new friends had heard of Nashotah House, and I was anxious for them to visit me and the seminary at which I taught. They accepted my invitation, and I awaited their arrival early one Sunday afternoon. Our plan was to tour our campus, have them meet some of my colleagues, attend Evensong, and end the evening with dinner at our house. As the Sunday afternoon in question passed and the hour of Evensong approached, I was much disturbed because my friends had not arrived. I was beginning to think they would not appear at all when they drove up, obviously in a great hurry, and offered their deepest apologies.

They said there had been an accident on the road and that they had stopped to "do something apostolic." They had stopped to minister to the injured, and then they had accompanied the ambulance to the hospital. How many Anglicans would have described such a ministry as "apostolic"?

God's Church is on a mission in the world, and it is an apostolic mission—a mission by persons to persons. The whole Church is apostolic; we are a people sent to people. Clergy are sent, that is to say, ordained, for their ordination is their sending, to remind the people of God that they are sent in the Son of God, who was sent by the Father. Any adequate definition of a Christian must, I believe, include the idea of being "sent by another to others." Christians are people who are sent to others no matter how they happen to feel at the moment! Our feelings have nothing to do with it. The mission is God's, not ours.

What are we sent to others to do? According to the words of the risen Christ himself, as recorded in Matthew's Gospel, we are to "make disciples of all nations. . ." (28:19).

Because we are to make disciples, we go as disciples. Disciples, not missiles. There is a big difference!

A disciple is someone who not only follows or knows about a master; a disciple is someone who has made the mind and will and teaching of the master his own. We cannot *make* the mind and will and teaching of Christ our own, but we can have the mind of Christ, do his will, and embrace his truth, if we accept the grace he offers us in the gift of his Spirit.

Christians are disciples who go filled with the presence of Another, not programmed for a target. The presence of God in us is our going, for in the presence of God we leave ourselves. I believe that truth is found in the words of our Lord himself when he said, "And he who sent me is with me; he has not left me alone, for I always do what is pleasing to him" (John 8:29). In those words, Jesus states his identity as the one sent by the Father. Jesus states that he always lives in the presence of the Father; he is never left alone; and, by doing what is always pleasing to the Father, Jesus leaves himself as the expression of the Father's will.

In considering the mission of the Church, I take it to be significant that the seventy, about whom we read in today's Gospel, were sent out two by two. The twelve were sent out by Jesus two by two also, as we read in the sixth chapter of Mark's Gospel (v. 7). Neither clergy or laity are lone rangers for God. We need the support of each other in order to make our witness and sustain our service in the world.

We are called together out of the world and sent together into the world (Ephes. 2:11-22; II Cor. 5:18). Our witness is credible only if we witness together, for we are called to be God's people, a nation, a race, a community. God chose himself a people, and individuals are saved by becoming members of God's people.

The Church is not made up of individuals who are saved one by one and then come together because they have salvation in common; salvation is reconciliation. We can become Christian only by Another with others! Mutual support and presence are of the essence of our witness and ministry. We cannot make a Christian witness alone, for the witness of a people is credible only if it is a common witness. We are a reconciled people; how can we leave each other out?

We are God's people, called to live in his kingdom, and to lead others into that kingdom. When Jesus sent the seventy out two by two, he told them to proclaim that "the kingdom of God has come near to you" (Lk. 10:9).

The kingdom is found where something new and good happens in people's lives. The apostolic mission of the Church is to witness to the newness of life in Christ by being the presence of that newness—the presence of Jesus in the power of the Spirit—in the world.

That is what we are sent to do. Our mission is to let ourselves *be sent*. Christian mission is apostolic mission; that is the Good News.

We are sent into the world by the Son, as the Son was sent into the world by the Father.

That is why the world has hope!

Sermon at the Festival Eucharist:
for St. Michael and All Angels

Jack C. Knight

*Surely the Lord is in this place, and I did not know
it. . . . How awesome is this place!*

(Genesis 28:16-17)

Today we celebrate three separate things in a single service.
First, we are honored to have our Presiding Bishop John
Maury Allin here with us, and to have the opportunity to
honor him for his labors on behalf of the entire Church as
we have moved across some new and uncharted territory.

Second, we honor Bishop Jackson Kemper in this culmi-
nation of several days of worship and lectures on the mission of the Church. In so doing, we pray that we might come
to value more highly those qualities of Christian service that
marked this apostle's life and which have continued to bear
fruit in the life of the Church.

Third, and last, we celebrate the feast of St. Michael and
All Angels, our traditional opening day of the school year
here at Nashotah.

There is a similarity and singleness of purpose in this
multifaceted celebration which I would like us to examine.
Let us begin with today's festival.

What kind of picture comes to your mind when you think
of St. Michael and all the angels? Is it the fluffy, feathered
creatures of considerable art, or the powerful world-famous
sculpture of St. Michael at the entrance of Coventry
Cathedral, or perhaps the rather unimpressive men in daz-
zling garments described in the Gospel of Luke? Whatever
the image, there is one thing which is common to all of them
and vital to our understanding of a missionary Church—
they were and are all messengers sent by God.

"Messenger"—this is the simple meaning of the word
"angel." And it is one with which we are familiar. If some-

one gives us a message which we are truly grateful to receive, our "thank you" may include the expression, "You're a real angel." So too, in this sense of the word, we are all called—whether layperson, bishop, priest or deacon—to be angels, messengers of the good news of God.

In the words of today's Gospel we hear that wonderful passage, "Behold, an Israelite indeed, in whom is no guile!" Of how many people could it be said, "Behold, a true man, a true woman, in whom is no deceit"?

Bishop Kemper was one such person.

In a book entitled, *An Apostle of the Western Church*, we are told of Jackson Kemper:

All of his best friends had long divined his fitness for the sacred ministry. The sweetness and evenness of his temper, the harmony of his talents, his unsullied purity of character and motive, and the unbroken course, from boyhood, of his Christian nurture, had already set him apart in their estimation. But he. . .with characteristic tenderness of conscience, hesitated. He shrank from the responsibility of a decision; he would leave it to divine direction.

His purity of motive and singleness of purpose is clearly seen in a Kemper quotation: "Our obligation is complete in one simple truth: This is the will of God."

The virtues attributed to Bishop Kemper will never go out of style, for they are the very buttresses of doing God's will in expanding his mission.

We too are to be without guile!

Nashotah House has taken its place in the role of the westward extension of the mission of the Church. There were hard times. Times that saw this institution brought near to the brink of failure. Cold, hunger and hard work were not strangers to those who were students here during the first decades of our life.

We think of the courage of those three young deacons—James Lloyd Breck, William Adams and John Henry Hobart—who responded to the call of Bishop Kemper to come West to help extend the mission of the Church on the frontier. Here they settled, and just a few feet from where we now stand they held the first Christian service of worship known to have taken place on these sacred grounds.

One has but to drive for miles and miles in any direction to see the fruit of their labor in this part of the Lord's vineyard and the results of Kemper's vision.

Today we are privileged to look back over 143 years in the life and work of this mission of the Church. But we are also called to look ahead to the future of the Church and to this seminary's role in providing a quality theological education for those who will labor on the front lines of the mission of the Church—the local congregation.

Yes, we are all to be messengers. And what is our message? It is not anything new or original. It is the timeless and ever fresh news that God is love—he loves each one of us so much that he sent his Son to live and die for us, to reconcile us to him—and since he loves each of us, we need to love one another.

Where are we to proclaim this message? Any street corner or doorway will do.

How will this be accomplished? This is the difficult part, and one which many will not want to hear. Still it has to be said. We, the Church, must offer the best we have. We must offer the best of our sons and daughters, the best years of our lives, and the best of our opportunities for someone else. We must not count the cost! We need only to know that in so giving we are doing God's will. This Kemper did. To this we also are called.

To know that courage has been present in times past can encourage us in the present. We must remember and believe that there is no epoch or season for giants in the faith. Giant vision makes for giant action. We are the recipients of an enlarged vision through Partners in Mission, through Venture in Mission and through Next Step in Mission. For this we rejoice and call upon God to insure that it be not just a valley in a far off land where a Jacob would cry out—or on a bluff overlooking Upper Nashotah Lake where the dean exclaims—"surely the Lord is in this place; his messengers abound." No, the whole of mankind, in every place, should take up in startled joy the refrain, "How awesome is this place!"

Conference Participants

John Maury Allin served as the twenty-third Presiding Bishop and first Primate of the Episcopal Church in the United States of America from 1974 to 1986. During his twelve-year tenure as chief pastor, the church launched Venture in Mission, a massive capital funds campaign aimed at renewing mission and ministry at the national, diocesan and parochial levels. He has challenged Episcopalians to be a mission-minded people, bold in witness and service.

V. Nelle Bellamy has been the Archivist of the Episcopal Church since 1959 and is adjunct Professor of Church History at the Episcopal Theological Seminary of the Southwest, Austin, Texas. She is a Fellow of the Society of American Archivists and has served on various archival and church commissions. Her latest publication is "Participation of Women in the Public Life of the Anglican Communion," in *Triumph over Silence: Women in Protestant History* (1985).

Nelson R. Burr, retired Librarian of Congress, is a director of the Historical Society of the Episcopal Church. Author of numerous works in the field of American religious history, his publication of *A Critical Bibliography of Religion in America,* two volumes (1961), is considered a landmark in American studies. He has lately completed *New Eden and New Babylon: Religious Thoughts of American Authors, A Bibliography.*

W. Roland Foster is professor of American Church History and Missiology at The General Theological Seminary, New York City, where he served as Dean from 1973 to 1978. He has published major works on the Scottish Reformation and is the author of *The Role of the Presiding Bishop* (1982). He is vice president of the Historical Society of the Episcopal Church and a member of the Standing Commission on World Mission of the General Convention.

Richard F. Grein, sometime Professor of Pastoral Theology at Nashotah House, was consecrated Bishop of Kansas in 1981. He is a member of the House of Bishops Committee on Pastoral Development, the General Board of Examining Chaplains, and a trustee of the National Center for the Diaconate. He is co-author of *Anglican Theology and Pastoral Care* (1985).

James E. Griffiss is William Adams Professor of Philosophical and Systematic Theology at Nashotah House. He is a member of the Theological Committee of the Standing Commission on Ecumenical Relations of the General Convention. He is author of *Church, Ministry, and Unity: A Divine Commission* (1983), and has lately edited and co-authored *Anglican Theology and Pastoral Care* (1985).

David L. Holmes, Professor of Religion at the College of William and Mary, Williamsburg, Virginia, is a member of the editorial board of the *Historical Magazine of the Protestant Episcopal Church*. He has published widely in the field of American church history and is author of *The Episcopalians,* a forthcoming volume in the new American Denomination Series.

Jack C. Knight became the sixteenth Dean and President of Nashotah House on July 1, 1985. He has been involved in mission throughout his ministry, having served as canon missioner in the dioceses of Colorado and Louisiana. He received the Bishop's Cross for Outstanding Service in the Diocese of Colorado in recognition of his work as chairman of the Committee on Mission Strategy and chairman of Venture in Mission.

Arthur A. Vogel is bishop of West Missouri. He was formerly Professor of Theology and Sub-Dean of Nashotah House. In 1969 he was appointed to the Anglican-Roman Catholic International Commission by the Archbishop of Canterbury, and is a member of ARCIC-II. He is the author of nine books, and the recent editor and co-author of *Theology in Anglicanism* (1984).

Roger J. White is the tenth Bishop of Milwaukee in succession to Jackson Kemper. His special interests are in the area of ministry development, mission strategy, parochial renewal and development, and ministry to urban areas. He is a contributor to *Realities and Visions: The Church's Mission Today* (1976).

J. Robert Wright is St. Mark's Church in the Bowerie Professor of Ecclesiastical History at The General Theological Seminary, New York City. He is a member of the Commission on Faith and Order of the World Council of Churches, the Standing Commission on Ecumenical Relations of the Episcopal Church and the Anglican-Roman Catholic International Commission. He has written extensively in the field of ecumenism, and is editor and co-author of *A Communion of Communions: One Eucharistic Fellowship* (1979).

Friends of a Missionary Church

Patrons

All Saints Church — Fort Worth, Texas
Cathedral Church of Saint Paul — Fond du Lac, Wisconsin
Christ Church Cathedral — Indianapolis, Indiana
Christ Church — Whitefish Bay, Wisconsin
Church of the Holy Comforter — Kenilworth, Illinois
Diocese of Milwaukee
Diocese of Northern Indiana
The Rt. Rev. Charles T. Gaskell — Milwaukee, Wisconsin
Nashotah House — Nashotah, Wisconsin
St. George's Church — Schenectady, New York
St. Michael and All Angels
Church — Denver, Colorado
Trinity Cathedral — Davenport, Iowa
The Rt. Rev. Robert C. Witcher — Diocese of Long Island
Zion Episcopal Church — Oconomowoc, Wisconsin

Sponsors

The Rev. John G. B. Andrew — New York, New York
Cathedral Church of St. James — Chicago, Illinois
Cathedral Church of St. Paul — Peoria, Illinois
Cathedral of All Saints — Albany, New York
Cathedral of Our Merciful Saviour — Faribault, Minnesota
Christ Church — Philadelphia, Pennsylvania
Christ Church — Delavan, Wisconsin
Christ Church — Green Bay, Wisconsin
Christ Church — LaCrosse, Wisconsin
Church of Gethsemane — Minneapolis, Minnesota
Church of St. Mary the Virgin — New York, New York
Church of St. Uriel the Archangel — Sea Girt, New Jersey
Diocese of Eau Claire
Diocese of Fond du Lac
Diocese of Indianapolis
Diocese of Kansas
Diocese of Minnesota
Diocese of Missouri
Diocese of West Missouri
Mr. Samuel R. Durand — Palo Alto, California
Grace and Holy Trinity Cathedral — Kansas City, Missouri
Grace Church — Sheboygan, Wisconsin

The Rev. Benjamin V. Lavey and	
Mrs. Anne H. Lavey	LaJolla, California
The Rev. Nicholas D. Pierce and	
Mrs. Louise S. Pierce	Peoria, Illinois
St. Boniface Church	Mequon, Wisconsin
Mr. Baldwin E. St. George	Sullivan, Wisconsin
St. James Church	Milwaukee, Wisconsin
St. John's Church	Keokuk, Iowa
St. John's Church	Dubuque, Iowa
St. Luke's Church	Baton Rouge, Louisiana
St. Matthew's Church	Kenosha, Wisconsin
St. Matthias Church	Waukesha, Wisconsin
St. Paul's Church	Norwalk, Connecticut
St. Paul's Church	Chatham, New Jersey
St. Stephen's Church	Terre Haute, Indiana
The General Theological Seminary	New York, New York
Trinity Church	Columbus, Georgia
Trinity Church	New York, New York

Contributors

The Rev. Robert O. Ahlenius and	
Mrs. Barbara A. Ahlenius	Chanute, Kansas
The Rev. Evan L. Ardley	Lafayette, Indiana
Ascension Church	Stillwater, Minnesota
The Rev. John C. Blakslee and	
Mrs. Helen E. Blakslee	South Holland, Illinois
The Rev. Robert G. Carroon	Hartford, Connecticut
Church of the Incarnation	Chesterton, Indiana
Church of St. John Chrysostom	Delafield, Wisconsin
Congregation of the Companions of	
the Holy Savior	
Harold J. Conlon, M.D.	Milwaukee, Wisconsin
Mr. Lawrence M. Crutcher	Greenwich, Connecticut
The Rev. James H. Davis	Manchester, Iowa
The Rev. Kenneth R. Dimmick	Shreveport, Louisiana
Mrs. Dorothea M. Engleman	Fort Worth, Texas
Mr. James W. Fender	Madison, Wisconsin
Miss Nora G. Frisbie	Claremont, California
The Rev. Charles E. N. Hoffacker	De Kalb, Illinois
Mr. William V. Kaeser and	
Mrs. Patricia S. Kaeser	Madison, Wisconsin
Mr. and Mrs. Jackson Kemper IV	Hawthorn Woods, Illinois
The Rev. Franklin J. Klohn	Dubuque, Iowa
Marie E. Leupold	Brookfield, Wisconsin
The Rev. Robert H. Limpert, Jr.	Brant Lake, New York
The Rev. John S. Macauley	Lawrence, Kansas

The Rev. Robert J. L. Matthews — Lawrence, Kansas
Mission Board, Nashotah House — Nashotah, Wisconsin
Mr. Frederick C. Philputt and
  Mrs. Nancy Philputt — Oconomowoc, Wisconsin
The Rev. Walter L. Prehn III — Dallas, Texas
St. Mark's Church — Barron, Wisconsin
St. Mary's Guild, Grace Church — Carthage, Missouri
St. Paul's Church — Milwaukee, Wisconsin
St. Simon's Church — Arlington Heights, Illinois
The Rev. Stephen Schaitberger and
  Mrs. Margaret M. Schaitberger — Brainerd, Minnesota
The Rev. Robert C. Snyder and
  Mrs. Mary A. Snyder — Eureka Springs, Arkansas
The Rev. Canon George C. Stacey — Milwaukee, Wisconsin
The Rev. James L. Steele — Morris, Illinois
Trinity Church — Bloomington, Indiana
The Rt. Rev. Roger J. White — Milwaukee, Wisconsin
The Rev. Clyde E. Whitney and
  Mrs. Rae Whitney — Scottsbluff, Nebraska
Mr. and Mrs. Loyal D. Wright — Francestown, New Hampshire